CARL JUNG AND ALCOHOLICS ANONYMOUS

CARL JUNG AND ALCOHOLICS ANONYMOUS

The Twelve Steps as a Spiritual Journey of Individuation

Ian McCabe

Routledge
Taylor & Francis Group

LONDON AND NEW YORK

First published 2015 by
Karnac Books Ltd.

Published 2018 by Routledge
2 Park Square, Milton Park, Abingdon, Oxon OX14 4RN
711 Third Avenue, New York, NY 10017, USA

Routledge is an imprint of the Taylor & Francis Group, an informa business

British Library Cataloguing in Publication Data

A C.I.P. for this book is available from the British Library

ISBN-13: 9781782203124 (pbk)

Typeset by V Publishing Solutions Pvt Ltd., Chennai, India

To Jenny, my present from Heaven!

CONTENTS

ACKNOWLEDGEMENTS

Firstly I must acknowledge the work of Ernest Kurtz, now sadly deceased for his book, *Not-God*, which is the definitive history of A.A., and upon whose shoulders I stood.

Grateful thanks to my friend and patient mentor Dr. Finbar O'Mahony for his unrelenting support in editing and contributing ideas and input to this book. From the very beginning Finbar has been a reliable and grounding mainstay in my studies. Thank you!

This book is based on my thesis, *The 12 Steps as a Spiritual Journey of Individuation*, and I am grateful to Tess Castleman for her encouragement, advice, and gentle guidance and for her many valuable comments especially for sharing her experience on the dynamics of group work in a Jungian context. Similarly my thanks to Dr. Gerold Roth for being the first person to encourage me to publish the thesis and for forwarding a copy of his thesis on the subject of alcoholism and groups. My thanks to Dr. Bob Hinshaw for studiously reading the thesis and for his supportive comments.

The idea for the book emanated during a conversation over coffee with Jungian analyst Carol Tripp, in Einsiedeln a decade ago—my thanks to Carol for activating, promoting, and encouraging the idea! I am indeed most indebted for the professional guidance and interest of

Michelle Mirza and Stephen D'Avria, A.A. Archivists in New York and their colleague Darlene Smith for permission to quote from A.A. World Services publications. The guidance of the A.A. Archivists in New York and Akron added enormously to the thesis. The Assistant A.A. Archivist, Jim Burns in Akron, Ohio, was especially helpful, not least for driving me around the A.A. sights of Akron. My grateful thanks to the Principal Archivist in Akron, Gail L. who was readily available at the end of the telephone for guidance and help in networking. One such networking introduction was to Jay who unselfishly gave of his time and resources. My thanks also to the Archivist at Stepping Stones Archives, Bedford Hills, for recommending and locating files and posting me on photocopies. My grateful thanks to Vicente de Moura, Archivists at the C. G. Jung Institute archives for answering several queries and for sending me relevant extracts related to Jung. My thanks to Dr. Ribi, Dr. James Bulman-May and Dr. Nada Ivanovic for their detailed and helpful remarks on the chapter that included paragraphs comparing recovery to the alchemical process.

Similarly, in relation to Jung's attitude to group process, my thanks to Dr. Robert Strubel for forwarding his paper on groups. Thank you to Debbie Lindenmeyer, a specialist addiction counsellor, for her sustained interest and her eloquent words of endorsement.

Thanks to John Hopping for accompanying me on my research trip to Akron, Ohio and for supplying a picture of the tombstone in the graveyard of Winchester Cathedral, Salisbury. A special thanks to all of the members of A.A. and other twelve-step programmes who took an interest and contributed to this thesis especially to Don, Tom, Nicholas, Lorcan, Senet, Heather, Phillip, and to David for also discussing the similarities of A.A. and Freemasonry.

A special thank you to the CG Jung Librarian, Julia, for her cheerfulness and ability to locate material from unknown places. Finally to the Administrators, Irene Fueter for being a repository of knowledge about the Jung Institute, Annette Jorgens for making "Solomonic" decisions, and Petra Brem for her "Herculean" capacity and efficiency and "Jobian" patience in answering so many queries so promptly and clearly. A special acknowledgment to my friend Hugh McFadden for applying his erudite skills in helping to edit the final draft of the manuscript. For proof-reading and commenting on the final draft of the manuscrip, my grateful thanks to my colleagues, Jennifer Barry, Margaret Daly, Claire Faughey, Rebecca Goddard, Michelle Kane, Sara Lavecchira, Sean Meehan, Rita Olokun and Orla Sheil.

My grateful thanks to the staff of Karnac, Cecily Blench, Rod Tweedy, and Constance Govindin for guiding the manuscript through the process of publication. A special thanks to the copy editor Kate Morris for her assiduousness in correcting the errors in the manuscript and making it fit for publication. Lastly I am indebted to Leonard Rosenbaum for the detailed index and especially for his selflessness in proofreading the manuscript. Of course, responsibility for any errors rests solely with myself.

Acknowledgments of copyright permission

I am most grateful to John D for allowing me to use his portrait of Bill Wilson in the Mayflower Hotel. To Simon Barwood, Media and Communications officer with Winchester Cathedral for permission to reprint the picture of the tombstone.

To the *Grapevine* magazine for permission to use the correspondence between Bill Wilson and Carl Jung and for the extract from the Grapevine edition of 1958. Also to the Grapevine for permission to reproduce the Preamble of A.A. To A.A. World Services for permission to quote from their publications, including *Alcoholics Anonymous* and the *Twelve Steps and Twelve Traditions*. Acknowledgement to the board of trustees of the magazine *Share* for allowing the use of excerpts from their magazines—much appreciated and my thanks to the anonymous contributors to the magazine. To Princeton University for permission to use excerpts from the collected works of Carl Jung and *Selected Letters of C. G. Jung, 1909–1961* and *C. G. Jung Letters*.

I am beholden to you all!

Ian McCabe,
Dublin

ABOUT THE AUTHOR

Ian McCabe, PhD, Psy.D., is a Chartered Psychologist, Associate Fellow of the British Psychological Society and a Zurich-trained child and adult Jungian Analyst. While training at the Haight Ashbury Alcohol Treatment Center in San Francisco he studied alcohol and drug abuse at the University of California, Berkeley, extension. He has worked as a Clinical Psychologist with Addiction Response Crumlin, Dublin and is the Managing Director of the Irish Charity, Jung Institute for Free Analysis for Children, and is also Clinical Director of alcoholcounselling.com.

ABBREVIATIONS

Alcoholics Anonymous = A.A.

Anonymous = Anon

Alcoholics Anonymous Archives, General Service Office, New York = AAA

Quotations are referenced according to year, Box and Reel number: AAA, year, Box 18, R 8

Collected Works of C. G. Jung = CW

Stepping Stones Archives, Bedford Hills, New York = Stepping Stones Archives

INTRODUCTION

This book explains the programme of Alcoholics Anonymous and the twelve steps principally through the writings of Carl Jung and the co-founder of A.A., Bill Wilson. The book is divided into six chapters; the first will feature the correspondence between Carl Jung and Bill Wilson from 1945 until Jung's death in 1961. The second part of the chapter will give an account of Bill's experiments with LSD. This will contain an examination of a controversial letter from Wilson to Jung asking for his comments about using LSD in the treatment of alcoholics.

The second chapter will follow Bill Wilson's attempts at recovery and include an account of his entering Towns Hospital, New York, to dry out. There he had a Pauline 'road to Damascus' type spiritual experience that transformed his life. This led him to decide to devote his life to helping fellow alcoholics. Six months later, in a moment of temptation he contacted another alcoholic, Dr. Bob Smith, who was to become the co-founder of A.A. This chapter explains how A.A. works and how the "Bible" of A.A., namely the "Big Book",[1] *Alcoholics Anonymous*, came to be written.

The third chapter will attempt to understand the illness of alcoholism from a medical and psychological perspective principally through the case notes of Carl Jung. His insightful and graphic descriptions are an excellent introduction to understanding the symptoms and behavioural problems associated with alcoholism.

Chapter Four will explain the short preamble of A.A., which contains the principles of how A.A. actually works. Also included in this chapter is an explanation of how A.A. meetings are organised and what happens inside an actual meeting.

The following chapter explains the twelve steps by means of personal stories from recovering members of A.A., and includes a Jungian perspective. Many of these stories involve alcoholics who, upon reaching their "rock bottom",[2] were startled by sudden spiritual moments of clarity. The programme of A.A. is then compared to Jungian analysis; in particular, this chapter will highlight the similarities of the Jungian journey of individuation and the A.A. spiritual awakening.

The final chapter will be devoted to explaining spiritual experiences and spiritual awakenings. This will include a narrative from William James's book, *The Varieties of Religious Experience*, from the nineteenth century that shows a direct link between a recovering alcoholic, Samuel Hadley, and the Episcopalian church in Manhattan where Bill Wilson first tasted sobriety.

This chapter will also examine the question of whether A.A. and Jungianism are cults. Even though this topic is outside the scope of this book, it will be addressed simply because both organisations are subject to the criticism that they are "cult-like".

The conclusion will discuss several topics including why A.A. works, its universal success, and Bill's research into LSD.

The appendices at the end of this book include the original correspondence between Carl Jung and Bill Wilson, the twelve steps, the twelve traditions, the twelve promises, and correspondence from Bill Wilson who shared his thoughts about his spiritual experience with a member of A.A. The final appendix reproduces a page of Wilson's second letter to Jung about using LSD to treat alcoholics.

CHAPTER ONE

Carl Jung and Bill Wilson 1945–1961

Communication between Bill Wilson and Carl Jung as mediated by their "Student", Margarita Luttichau

The correspondence between Bill Wilson and Carl Jung dates back to 1945. This was made possible through Margarita Luttichau[1] who acted as an intermediary between both men. She was a student of Carl Jung and was also a protégé of Bill Wilson. Effectively she was mentored by both men. She travelled between America and Switzerland and in letters and conversations made each man aware of the words, writings, and ideas of the other. Margarita was interested in applying the format and principles of A.A. group work to "general neurotics". In the summer of 1945, Margarita gave Bill Wilson a copy of Jung's book, *Modern Man in Search of a Soul*. Bill wrote to her at the beginning of October 1945:

> You must know the memory of our chat together at Nantucket comes back often and most pleasantly and I am very grateful for that book you handed me, not only does it confirm fragmentary impressions I had of Dr. Jung—it reveals him as a truly great man. His feeling for people, his real humility, his capacity for synthesis

1

in a field still so confused—these qualities in him are delightful to observe …. I hope the A.A. book I sent you on my return here did not go astray. (AAA, 1945, Box 18, R 8)

In November 1945 Margarita met with Jung in Zurich and talked to him about Bill Wilson. She showed him "bits of printed matters I had along" about A.A.

She replied to Wilson's letter in early December 1945:

> Jung was perfectly fascinated and wanted to know a lot more. Of course I told him about the neurotics who were turning to you too and I felt that you should both talk the matter over to see if there was any such way as the A.A. might open up in other countries. (AAA, 1945, Box 18, R 8)

Interestingly, given Jung's reputed disdain for groups, Margarita also recorded that, "He was deeply interested and said he was sure only some such solution whereby a great many people could receive help could possibly erase the terrible need of to-day" (Ibid.). Margarita planned to talk further with Jung when he had read over the A.A. literature. She ended her letter:

> I have very often thought about that wonderful Saturday in New York and I want to thank you again most warmly. Please give my greetings and best wishes to your wife and to all friends I met at the party. (Ibid.)

A month later on 10 January 1946, Wilson sent a three-page letter to Margarita in which he contrasts the understanding of neurosis by Freudians and Jungians. Essentially Freud was an atheist whereas Jung, whose father and uncles were church ministers, included the spiritual aspect in his psychology.

Wilson began his letter, "Dear Margarita, your long and fascinating letter was received with the greatest pleasure" (AAA, 1946, Box 18, R 8). He wrote that he had "read and re-read" the book *Modern Man in Search of a Soul*.

> Building upon Freud's pioneering, Dr. Jung comes to very different conclusions about diagnosis, treatment, composition of the personality and man's place in the cosmos. Dr. Jung seems capable

of open-mindedness, a capacity for sympathetic constructions that appears pretty much lacking in Freud. He seems to be a truly great man. I would much like to meet him someday. (Ibid.)

Wilson told Margarita that he had been reading Freud's book, *Introduction to Psychoanalysis*:

> That he is reported to have died a gloomy old man I can understand. Hoisted by his own petard … . I cannot resist the conclusion that the philosophical implications arising from Freud's work have done a great deal to poison modern thought. Many people are constantly coming into A.A. who have been under treatment by Freudians. Their reactions are interesting. The most common one is ridiculing any and all psychiatrists. Of course this is unfair and unfortunate. That is the impression they have.
>
> Then we have the type that seems to have been shattered by treatment instead of healed. Believing what psychiatry has told him about himself he cannot "take it". He is more miserable than ever. Then we have the third and very interesting type of Freudian patient. These are apt to be sold on Freud in the sense that adherents of a religion worship their founder. They brook no questioning or doubt. They say, "It is so because the master says so". They venerate Freud as a great debunker of the human race. These people realise they are strong enough to take their own debunking. They beat on their chests, as it were, crying, "our heads are bloody, but unbowed". They tend to be atheists, cynical, ruthlessly competitive and hard as nails. Politically they are apt to admire Communists.

Bill continued,

> Of course I haven't too much basis for these observations. As a newcomer in the field I really have no right to make them at all. There is bound to be a great deal of bias, because in A.A. we see only the failures of psychiatry. Then, to, [sic] most of the people we get in have been treated by Freudians. But it is also true, that after coming into A.A., many who have received psychiatric treatment report that they are able to go back over the experience and pick out of it much that is helpful. (Ibid.)

Wilson also asked Margarita to remind Jung that it was a former patient of his, Rowland Hazard, "an alcoholic ... who when associated with the Oxford Group[2] here in New York helped me very much with my own recovery" (Ibid.).

On 2 September 1947, Margarita wrote to Bill about "a long talk" she had had with Jung during a conference on analytical psychology in Ascona, Switzerland. Her letter refers to Jung's antipathy to group work: "As well I knew he is interested in the forming of an individual not in group work—but after hearing the whole thing he was very interested and gave me extraordinarily complete instructions how it might be managed" (AAA, 1947, Box 18, R 8).

A month later, in October 1947, Wilson replied to Margarita's letter, "I was delighted with your account of your meeting with Dr. Jung and am encouraged that he thinks there might be something to the group method with neurotics—though the contrary opinion seems still to prevail" (Ibid.).

Earlier in March 1947, Wilson wrote to a friend in Washington, D.C. asking her to assist Margarita in finding accommodation when visiting there. He commentated that "she is one of the few persons holding a personal endorsement from Dr. Carl Jung." (AAA, 1947, Box 18, R8)

> It was my friend Margarita who first carried the news of AA to Dr. Jung who at once showed an intense- even an excited interest. He expressed the hope that AA methods could finally play a great part in the general field of neurosis—that it might have a far wider scope than alcohol. (Ibid.)

Wilson explained that Margarita wanted to set up her own private practice and he said he was "intensely interested, partly because of my own severe experience with depression." Wilson explained that Margarita wanted to "participate as one of us in some experimental group work on neurosis", and when she returns to New York "we have in mind starting a group of neurotics of which I shall surely be candidate number one." He ended his letter with a personal approval of Margarita:

> Though not an alcoholic, Margarita is qualified as "one of us". She has known the most acute mental suffering for which she has been freed by Dr. Jung plus her own spiritual resources which, by the way, are great. (Ibid.)

From this triangular correspondence involving Wilson, Jung, and Margarita we can see the development of their belief that the format and principles of A.A. were capable of being extended to many neuroses and other addictions. Since then the twelve steps of A.A. have been extended to many other problems and today there exists twelve step programmes for abuse survivors, anorexia and bulimia, anxiety and depression, phobics, and financial problems. The twelve-step programme transferred seamlessly to other addictions so today there exists: Narcotics Anonymous, Workaholics Anonymous, Sexaholics Anonymous, Gamblers Anonymous, Cocaine Anonymous, Marijuana Anonymous, Nicotine Anonymous, Co-Dependents Anonymous, and Pills Anonymous.

Carl Jung's attitude to applying A.A. group work to "general neurotics"

Jung reputedly believed that groups stifle the individuation process. Jungian analyst Dr. Robert Strubel writes "It would be wrong, however, to pin Jung down to such a bias without considering his other statements on this subject" (p. 2 of the original article kindly forwarded by Robert Strubel, reproduced in Beebe, 1983).

The correspondence between Margarita Luttichau and Bill Wilson supports the proposition that Jung was flexible enough to endorse group work. The proof of the success of Alcoholics Anonymous in using a group method was the reason why Jung was so receptive to Margarita Luttichau's ideas about adapting group work to "general neurotics". Jung had in fact been quite critical of group psychology; he believed that any transformations experienced in groups did not last. He wrote:

> To experience transformation in a group and to experience it in oneself are two totally different things. If any considerable group of persons are united and identified with one another by a particular frame of mind, the resultant transformation experience bears only a very remote resemblance to the experience of individual transformation. (CW 9i, para. 225)

Jung also believed that transformation in a group was "also much easier to achieve, because the presence of so many people together exerts great suggestive force. The individual in a crowd easily becomes the victim of his own suggestibility" (CW 9i, para. 225).

Jung was aware that Hitler had mesmerised groups at the pre-war Nazi rallies in Nuremberg. Jung disliked groups because he believed that a group would sink to the level of the consciousness of that of its lowest member.

> The total psyche emerging from the group is below the level of the individual psyche. If it is a large group, the collective psyche will be more like the psyche of an animal, which is the reason why the ethical attitude of large organisations is always doubtful. (CW 9i, para. 225)

Paradoxically, while the quoted words of Jung are generally critical of groups, they are actually supportive of the organisational structure of A.A. group meetings. For example when he states that if change happens in a group

> the group experience goes no deeper than the level of one's own mind in that state. It does work a change in you, but the change does not last. On the contrary you must have recourse to mass intoxication in order to consolidate the experience and your belief in it. (CW 9i para. 226)

Jung's belief that change in a group does not last is exemplified by evangelical meetings. Indeed Bill Wilson, inspired by Ebby Thacher, first attended a meeting of the evangelical Oxford Group in Calvary Church and went forward and swore off alcohol but was drinking the following day. For change to become permanent people need to replicate the same feeling through regular attendances at such meetings. This need to attend meetings regularly to keep the inspirational feeling alive validates the need for people who achieved sobriety through the support of an A.A. group to continuously attend meetings. A person who recovers owes their sobriety to the support of the group and generally in order to maintain sobriety they need the continuous support of the fellowship of A.A. and its twelve-step programme. This is the reason they need to "keep coming back" to the meetings.

Jung surprisingly does offer an encouraging note about groups:

> There are also positive experiences, for instance, a positive enthusiasm which spurs the individual to noble deeds or an equally

positive feeling of human solidarity. Facts of this kind should not be denied. The group can give the individual courage, a bearing, and a dignity which may easily get lost in isolation. It can awaken within him the memory of being a man among men. (CW 9i, para. 228)

The importance of the A.A. group as a means of support for alcoholics is referred to in an unpublished thesis by Dr. Gerold Roth, a psychiatrist working in the field of addiction. The results of his research shows that attendance at A.A. does not simply cause an addiction shift, but often leads to actual behaviour changes (Personal communication, 28 January 2013).

Therapeutic work in groups can be very effective as it builds up a common humanitarian bond and indeed can activate the collective unconscious. Today there are many different groups for "neurotics" that are based or patterned on the twelve steps of A.A., most prominently the group AWARE that offers group support for people with depression (aware.ie). It should be noted that pioneering work is being accomplished by some Jungian analysts who work very successfully with groups in analysing dreams (Castleman, 2009). However, Jung was correct in stating that groups do naturally look for scapegoats and can bully individual members as exemplified in Dr. Arthur Colman's book, *Up From Scapegoating* (Colman, 1995).

Bill Wilson's first letter to Carl Jung, 1961

Bill wrote two letters to Jung and several to his secretary, Aniela Jaffe. The first letter was dated 23 January 1961 (see Appendix One). Wilson attached a cover letter to Aniela Jaffe,[3] "enclosing a letter that should have been sent to Dr. Jung long ago. As you will see, it deals with the very important part he played in the forming of Alcoholics Anonymous" (Letter to Jaffe is also dated 23 January, 1961, Stepping Stones Archives). In his letter to Jung, Wilson wrote that according to his recollection a former patient of Jung, Rowland Hazard, who was being treated for alcoholism, had a relapse and revisited Jung in 1931 (actually it was 1926, see Bluhm, 2006). Wilson reminded Jung of the conversation he had with Hazard:

> First of all, you frankly told him of his hopelessness, so far as any
> further medical or psychiatric treatment might be concerned. This
> candid and humble statement of yours was beyond doubt the first

foundation stone upon which our Society has since been built. (see Appendix One)

Wilson continued:

> When he then asked you if there was any other hope, you told him that there might be, provided he could become the subject of a spiritual or religious experience—in short, a genuine conversion. You pointed out how such an experience, if brought about, might remotivate him when nothing else could. But you did caution, though, that while such experiences had sometimes brought recovery to alcoholics, they were, nevertheless, comparatively rare. You recommended that he place himself in a religious atmosphere and hope for the best. This I believe was the substance of your advice. (Ibid.)

Upon his return to America, Rowland joined the Oxford Group, which helped him to stop drinking temporarily (Kurtz, 1991, p. 9). Later Rowland Hazard convinced Ebby Thacher to stop drinking, who in turn introduced Bill to the Oxford Group where he gained sobriety at the end of 1934.

Wilson ended his letter by commending Jung's role in the formation of A.A. "Please be certain that your place in the affection, and in the history, of our Fellowship is like no other". Wilson always acknowledged that Jung's advice to Hazard "set Alcoholics Anonymous in motion" (Anon, 2000, p. 125). While Jung's advice to Hazard was an important link in the chain of events that led to the founding of Alcoholics Anonymous, Wilson did credit others, including William James as being amongst the founders of A.A. (Anon, 1991b, p. 124).

However Wilson's acknowledgment of Jung's contribution to the formation of A.A. was not an impulsive ingratiating gesture; he had included this opinion fifteen years earlier in a letter to Margarita Luttichau. Referring to the advice Jung had given to Rowland Hazard and how it had influenced himself; he wrote humorously, "So you see, I could claim to be a lineal descendant from Dr. Jung. And this is far more comforting to think about than though I were descended from Freud" (L.D. 10 January 1946, Box 18, R 8). This may have been a reference to the fact that Rowland Hazard first applied to be a patient of Freud's but he was too busy, so Rowland then went to see Jung (Bluhm: See also, Jung, 1985, pp. 141–142).

Jung's reply to Wilson's letter

Jung replied to Wilson's letter seven days later on 30 January 1961 (see Appendix One). After thanking Bill for his letter Jung then referred to Rowland Hazard, writing that he had, "often wondered what had been his fate". Jung wrote that his talk with Roland [sic] was "based on the result of many experiences with men of his kind". Jung hinted about the difficulties he was under at that time, "I could not tell him everything" because in "those days I had to be exceedingly careful of what I said. I had found out that I was misunderstood in every possible way". Jung explained that this caution extended to Rowland Hazard, "Thus I was very careful when I talked to Roland H". Jung explained that the reason he could not give a full explanation to Rowland was because Jung identified the nature of Rowland's illness as spiritual.

Jung continued, "His craving for alcohol was the equivalent on a low level of the spiritual thirst of our being for wholeness, expressed in medieval language, the union with God". Jung was explaining that alcohol was a short cut to achieving a false spiritual experience. He added, "The only right and legitimate way to such an experience is, that it happens to you in reality and it can only happen to you when you walk on a path, which leads you to higher understanding" (Ibid.). This viewpoint of Jung's in relation to how a spiritual experience is achieved is noteworthy given that Wilson's follow-up letter dated 20 March 1961 advocated the use of LSD to introduce alcoholics in denial to an "instant" transcendent experience (Appendix Six).

Jung in his letter, further explained that his understanding was that there was evil in the world and perhaps for some people alcohol is an evil, "a depraving poison".

Jung wrote that he was

> strongly convinced that the evil principle prevailing in this world leads the unrecognized spiritual need into perdition, if it is not counteracted either by real religious insight or by the protective wall of human community. An ordinary man, not protected by an action from above and isolated in society, cannot resist the power of evil, which is called very aptly the Devil.

Jung had already written in 1957 about the vulnerability of people who have no guiding spiritual resource and titled a chapter of his book,

The Undiscovered Self, "The plight of the individual in modern society". In this book he elaborated and stated his belief that "The individual who is not anchored in God can offer no resistance on his own resources to the physical and moral blandishments of the world" (Jung, 1974, p. 24).

In his letter to Bill Wilson, Jung rhetorically asked, "How could one formulate such an insight that is not misunderstood in our days?" (Jung, Letter to Bill Wilson, 1961). And as though taking stock of the "risk" he was taking in referring to matters of spirituality, even in the early sixties, he then wrote, "But the use of such words arouses so many mistakes that one can only keep aloof from them as much as possible" (Ibid.).

While Jung's spiritual advice may seem acceptable today, in the twenties and thirties Jung was being assailed by the psychiatric and psychoanalytical professions who were not concerned with the healing power of spirituality. The psychiatric and psychoanalytical professions at that time were trying to gain scientific credibility for their methods and attempts to bridge spirituality and psychology were anathema to practitioners. Any indication by Jung that he was offering his patients "religious" advice or that he recognised a spiritual deficit in his patients would give grounds for him to be ridiculed. Even today, the term "religious or spiritual problem" only made it into a sub-section of the most recent edition of the psychiatrists' and psychologists' "bible", namely the *Diagnostic and Statistical Manual of Mental Disorders* (DSM-5). The term was placed in the category of "Other conditions that may be the focus of clinical attention" (American Psychiatric Association, 2013, p. 725).

In the mid-thirties in America, physicians were reluctant to treat alcoholics. In 1935, two years after the end of Prohibition, the American Medical Association (AMA), reputedly pronounced that alcoholism was a "moral failing" that was not responsive to conventional medical treatment. The AMA concluded that alcoholics were guilty of moral turpitude and this was a self-inflicted malady and thus alcoholics were responsible for their own condition and attempts to treat them were a waste of time for doctors! The AMA did not suggest any alternatives for curing alcoholism. There is a coincidence about the timing of the foundation of Alcoholics Anonymous in 1935 in that it could be viewed as a compensation that filled the vacuum left by the American medical establishment.

Although Jung mentioned in his letter to Wilson that he had "often wondered" about the fate of Rowland Hazard, there is a reference in his autobiography, *Memories, Dreams, Reflections* (Jung, 1985), to a patient or perhaps a composite of several patients, who are similar to Rowland. For example there is a reference to an American colleague who sent a patient to Jung with the diagnosis of incurable "alcohol neurasthenia". The doctor had also advised the patient to see a "neurological authority in Berlin, for he expected that my attempt at therapy would lead to nothing" (Jung, 1985, pp. 141–142). Coincidently, Rowland was first advised to see Freud in Vienna, but Freud was too busy, so Rowland then visited the next most world-renowned psychiatrist, Carl Jung (Bluhm). There is a second reference by Jung to a patient who is even more similar to Rowland, "when a member of the Oxford Group comes to me in order to get treatment, I say, 'You are in the Oxford Group; so long as you are there, you settle your affair with the Oxford Group. I can't do it better than Jesus'" (CW 18, para. 620).

Related to this is the following case presentation that Jung gave:

> A hysterical alcoholic was cured by this group movement, and they used him as a sort of model and sent him all round Europe, where he confessed so nicely and said he had done wrong and how he had got cured through the group movement. And when he had repeated his story twenty, or it may have been fifty times, he got sick of it and took to drink again. The spiritual sensation had simply faded away. Now what are they going to do with him? They say, now he is pathological, he must go to a doctor. See, in the first stage he has been cured by Jesus, in the second by a doctor! I should and did refuse such a case. I sent that man back to those people and said, "If you believe that Jesus has cured this man, he will do it a second time. And if he can't do it, you don't suppose that I can do it better than Jesus?" But that is just exactly what they do expect: when a man is pathological, Jesus won't help him but the doctor will. (CW 18, para. 621)
>
> As long as a fellow believes in the Oxford Group movement, he stays there; and as long as a man is in the Catholic Church, he is in the Catholic Church for better or worse and he should be cured by those means. And mind you, I have seen that they can be cured by those means—that is a fact! Absolution, the Holy Communion, can cure them, even in very serious cases. (CW 18, para. 622)

Jung's reference to a group who praise publicly someone for their temperance is a parody but carries a serious message in that anyone who is recognised by the public as a recovering alcoholic and a member of A.A. and then relapses does by association reduce people's confidence in the efficacy of the A.A. programme. Perhaps, it was similar carica- tures of "famous" people who had slips in their prostelysing recovery that encouraged A.A. to develop the concept of anonymity at the level of press, radio, and films. The principle of anonymity encourages mem- bers to adhere to the spiritual principles of A.A. rather than allowing their egos to feed off media publicity about how wonderful they are in having achieved sobriety.

Bill Wilson's experiments with LSD

Within A.A. headquarters there is still a great deal of protectiveness surrounding Bill's second letter to Jung. This is because the third page of Bill's letter refers to his advocacy of treating alcoholics, who were having difficulty with the spiritual aspect of the programme, with LSD. According to Kurtz, "Wilson's main efforts outside A.A. in the final fif- teen years of his life were attempts to remove the mental or psychologi- cal and physical obstacles that impeded some persons from openness to the spiritual" (Kurtz, 1991, p. 137).

Abram Hoffer, a biochemist and professor of psychiatry, and Humphrey Osmond, a psychiatrist, co-authored a book about using LSD to treat alcoholics, titled *New Hope for Alcoholics* (Hoffer & Osmond, 1968). They accidently stumbled upon LSD as a treatment for alcoholics. Originally, they were using LSD for treating schizophrenics and thought it induced "something very similar to delirium tremens" (Anon, 1991b, p. 369). As a form of Pavlovian behaviour training, they thought it would be a good idea to create a state of delirium tremens in alcoholics as a warning to them. Instead, somewhat amusingly, alcoholics actually enjoyed the LSD experience and reported that instead of being terrified by delirium tremens they found the experience "illuminating" (Ibid.). Hoffer and Osmond then realised that LSD could initiate alcoholics into having a spiritual experience that could help them stop drinking. Their book cites several case studies of alcoholics successfully being treated with LSD. Hoffer told Bill Wilson about these results and initially "he was extremely unthrilled. He was very much against giving alcoholics drugs" (Ibid.).

However, Wilson was impressed by the success rate Hoffer and Osmond were having which was much higher than that of A.A. Wilson hoped that if LSD could produce an experience of transcendence in the alcoholic then they would see that by using alcohol they were "using the wrong chemical to that end" (Kurtz, 1991, p. 136). That is, by using alcohol they were trying to gain a low-grade spiritual experience.

Bill Wilson investigated further and became a patient of Abram Hoffer. He took LSD in 1956, when it was legal, in the Veterans Administration Hospital in Los Angeles under the medical supervision of psychiatrist Sidney Cohen (Lattin, 2012, p. 195). According to his long-term secretary Nell Wing, "He had an experience that was totally spiritual, like his initial spiritual experience" and "far from keeping his activities a secret, he was eager to spread the word" (Quoted in Anon, 1991b, p. 371). Even though his wife Lois had a heart condition he persuaded her to take LSD and reported that she "is undergoing a very great general improvement since even this mild administration" (Ibid., p. 372). Bill was a salesman and had obviously sold himself on the benefits of LSD. However, Lois herself reported, "Bill gave me some. Actually, I could not tell any difference. I don't know. I looked down, and I saw things that were clearer, but they weren't any greener—it's supposed to make your perception greater. But I'd always been an observer of nature anyway and looked carefully at things" (Ibid.). From this it might appear that Bill was a blind advocate of LSD, but he was not a dogmatist and later wrote, "Of course, the convictions I now have are still very much subject to change" (Ibid., p. 375).

In 1957, Wilson wrote to Gerald Heard, a prominent philosopher and writer, about the personal psychological benefits he had gained from using LSD; he referred to the alleviation of his depression and his greater awareness and keener appreciation of beauty (Lattin, 2012, p. 183).

In June 1958, Wilson wrote a long letter outlining his positive views on LSD to Reverend Sam Shoemaker (Minister of the Calvary Church where he first gained sobriety) (Anon, 1991b, pp. 373–375). Bill believed that LSD might help alcoholics and in this letter Bill outlined his case for using LSD with alcoholics:

> I've taken lysergic acid several times, and have collected considerable information about it. The public is today being led to believe that LSD is a new psychiatric toy of awful dangers. It induces schizophrenia, they say. Nothing could be further from the truth … In the course of three or four years, they (Hoffer and Osmond) have

administered LSD to maybe 400 people of all kinds. Extensive tape recordings have been taken. The cases have been studied from the biochemical, psychiatric, and spiritual aspects. Again no record of any harm, no tendency to addiction. They have also found that there is no physical risk whatsoever. The material is about as harmless as aspirin. It was with them I took my first dose two years ago. (Ibid.)

Bill also wrote that he thought that:

The probability that prayer, fasting, meditation, despair, and other conditions that predispose one to classic mystical experiences do have their chemical components. The chemical conditions aid in shutting out the normal ego drives, and to that extent, they do open the doors to a wider perception. (Ibid.)

Bill warned prophetically LSD should,

Only be used for research purposes, it would certainly be a huge misfortune if it ever got loose in the general public without a careful preparation as to what the drug is and what the meaning of its effects may be. (Ibid.)

LSD did get "loose in the general public". Timothy Leary, a Harvard psychology lecturer, had approached Bill asking to be included in the work Bill was doing with LSD. While Bill had the good sense not to include Leary, he did write to him in 1961 saying that Aldous Huxley had "referred enthusiastically to your work … though LSD and some kindred alkaloids have had an amazingly bad press, there seems no doubt (about) their immense and growing value" (Lattin, 2010, p. 67). Leary then went on to encourage vulnerable young seekers to "turn on, tune in, drop out".

While many of the "hippy generation" mis-used LSD and took it in conjunction with illicit drugs to increase their "highs", there is no doubt that the media engaged in a frenzy of propaganda connecting LSD to suicide and permanent insanity. Had Bill become associated with Leary it probably would have done inestimable harm to the reputation of A.A. In this light, given the American government's fear and knee-jerk condemnation of LSD, one can appreciate the decision of the trustees of A.A. to distance themselves from Bill's association with LSD.

It is clear that Bill Wilson experimented with LSD because he was seeking still further ways of helping alcoholics, of helping specifically those alcoholics who could not seem to attain sobriety in A.A. because they could not "get the spiritual". Writing in the A.A. magazine, *Grapevine* in April 1961, Bill commented that, "Though three hundred thousand did recover in the last twenty-five years, maybe half a million more have walked into our midst, and then out again". Wilson may have had a sense of frustration that more could have been done to help these people who came looking for an answer. According to his wife Lois, "Bill's great hope was that continued research would find a means whereby those thousands of alcoholics who want to stop drinking but are too ill to grasp the A.A. program could be released from their bondage and enabled to join A.A." (Kurtz, 1991, p. 358, fn 7).

It was from this background and his own experience of taking LSD that Wilson, somewhat naively, wrote his second letter to Carl Jung in March 1961 asking for his comments on the use of LSD for alcoholics. As we shall see it is obvious that Bill Wilson was not aware of Jung's dogmatic antagonism to the use of LSD: Jung considered LSD to be similar to mescaline, and he thought the usage of psychedelic mind-expanding drugs to be a short cut to a genuine spiritual experience.

Bill Wilson's second letter to Carl Jung about LSD

Bill's second letter of 20 March 1961, began by thanking him and assuring him of confidentiality (Anon, 1991b, pp. 385–386). It included an appreciation of Jung's understanding that alcoholism was associated with a spiritual search. Wilson continued to give a favourable synopsis of Jung's book *Modern Man in Search of a Soul.*[4] The letter also suggested the possibility of measuring psychic phenomena with modern equipment. Perhaps the most relevant and controversial part of the letter was Bill's request to Jung for a comment on the use of lysergic acid diethylamide (LSD) to assist alcoholics achieve a spiritual experience (see Appendix Six).

> Dear Dr. Jung:
>   Your affecting letter has been received with much gratitude. Because in feeling and view it so completely reinforces the

outlook of most thoughtful A.A. members, it will be a treasured possession always ....

Years ago some of us read with great benefit your book entitled "Modern Man in Search of a Soul". You observe, in effect, that most persons having arrived at age 40 and having acquired no conclusions of as to who they were, or where they were, or where they were going next in the Cosmos, would be bound to encounter increasing neurotic difficulties ....

These views of yours, Doctor, had an immense impact upon some of the early members of our A.A. fellowship. We saw that you had perfectly described the impasse in which we had once been, but from which we had been delivered through our several spiritual awakenings. This "spiritual experience" had to be our key to survival and growth. We saw that the alcoholic's helplessness could be turned to vital advantage. By the admission of this, he could be deflated at depth, thus fulfilling the first condition of a re-motivating conversion experience.

So the forgoing is still another example of your great helpfulness to us of A.A. in our formative period ....

You spoke a language of the heart that we could understand. (Anon 1991b, pp. 385–386. Copy in Stepping Stones Archives)

Wilson was presumably aware of Jung's interest in séances, telepathy, and the paranormal. His letter put forward the idea that human consciousness after death might be measured using modern scientific instruments. The archives in Stepping Stones, the former home of Bill Wilson, contain extensive written notes on the regular séances which took place in a small ground floor room there.

On the last page of his three-page letter he broached the issue of using LSD to help still suffering alcoholics. (Appendix V1) Bill believed that a transcendent LSD experience would be sufficient to convince alcoholics in denial that there was a spiritual component to their mind. He wrote that despite some psychiatrists thinking that LSD experiences are related to schizophrenia he was sure that was rarely the case. Bill referred to his own use of LSD and felt that it put him more in touch with reality and believed that it is harmless and non-addictive.

Bill then referred to Hoffer and Osmond's research studies at the University of Saskatchewan, Canada. They had conducted research on using LSD for alcoholism and claimed a recovery of fifty per cent. Bill claimed that he was aware of 50,000 administrations of LSD in the US and Canada, barely none of which had resulted in damage while the overwhelming majority had benefited the participants. Bill ended his letter by asking Jung to comment on his remarks (Ibid.).

Wilson's letter was acknowledged by Aniela Jaffe; writing on 5 May 1961, she explained to Wilson that it was ill-health that prevented the eighty-six-year-old Jung from replying to his letter:

> Carl Jung read your letter of March 20th. He had in his mind to answer you, but that he fell ill and the doctor ordered complete rest. Feeling better he left for a long vacation and therefore the mail is not done. Maybe he will write you at a later time.

Jaffe added a postscript, "He said that he is very much interested in the work of Alcoholics Anonymous" (Stepping Stones Archives).

Wilson replied to Jaffe on 25 May:

> As you know, I sent him a considerable batch of material about Alcoholics Anonymous and my last letter posed questions which he may neither have the time or energy to answer. So I add my concern to yours that he not be burdened unduly. (Stepping Stones Archives)

Jung died twelve days later on 6 June 1961.

Jaffe's letter was a courteous explanation and was most likely true, especially given that the last recorded letter in the selected letters of *C. G. Jung Letters, Vol 2, 1951–1961,* was dated 10 March 1961. This indicates that Jung wrote his last letter at least a couple of weeks before receiving Bill Wilson's second letter which included a request for a comment on the question of prescribing LSD to alcoholics.

It is also possible, though probably less likely, that Jung did not want to disagree with Wilson because as we shall see later he had his own strong views on the subject of psychedelic drugs, Peyote, and Mescaline.

Jung's views on psychedelic drugs: peyote, mescaline, and LSD

Frank McLynn, an astute biographer of Jung's work, wrote that the only benefit Jung saw in LSD was that it could introduce and convince people of the existence of the unconscious. McLynn believes that Jung would have considered that LSD could do no more than what active imagination could achieve, though without the hard psychological work entailed! According to McLynn, Jung feared that taking LSD could "release a latent psychosis" (McLynn, 1997, p. 519).

Jung wrote several letters in relation to the drugs peyote, mescaline, and LSD. The first in April 1954, was to Victor Francis White, a Dominican priest and long-term correspondent of Jung. White had written to Jung him about his visit to "Worcestershire asylum" to talk to staff and "try to lend a hand with religious archetypal material which patients were producing under the LSD drug" (Jung-White letters, p. 231). On 10 April 1954, Jung replied at length and asked:

> Is the LSD-drug mescaline? It has indeed very curious effects— *vide* Aldous Huxley—of which I know far too little. I don't know either what its psychotherapeutic value with neurotic or psychotic patients is. I only know there is no point in wishing to know more of the collective unconscious than one gets through dreams and intuition …. (Adler & Jaffe, 1976, p. 172)

Jung then waxed poetically:

> I should hate the thought that I had touched on the sphere where the paint is made that colours the world, where the light is created that makes shine the splendour of the dawn, the lines and shapes of all forms, the sound that fills the orbit, the thought that illuminates the darkness of the void …. I am profoundly mistrustful of the "pure gifts of the Gods." You pay very dearly for them. (Adler & Jaffe, 1976, pp. 172–173)

Jung thought Aldous Huxley, who was an advocate of LSD, was mistaken in advocating LSD: "He does not know that he is in the role of the 'Zauberlehrling' [*sorcerer's apprentice*, my italics] who learned from his master how to call the ghosts but did not know how to get rid of them again" (Adler & Jaffe, 1976, p. 172).

It is curious that Jung does not mention the possible therapeutic effects of LSD, especially since thirty years previously he was "acquainted" with the research work on mescaline by a German Psychiatrist, Dr. Hans Prinzhorn, "and thus I had ample opportunity to learn about the effects of the drug as well as about the nature of the psychic material involved in the experiment" (L.D. 15 February 1955, in Jung, 1976). Additionally it is worth noting the coincidence that LSD was discovered accidentally a decade earlier by a Swiss chemist, Albert Hoffman, in Basle in 1943. Ian Baker's unpublished thesis gives the background to the accidental discovery of LSD and the experimental research with LSD in Zurich.[5]

In his book, *Distilled Spirits*, Don Lattin gives a detailed history of the emergence of the psychedelic culture in California in the mid-fifties. He recounts how Bill Wilson first took LSD under the guidance of psychiatrist, Dr. Sidney Cohen and clinical psychologist, Betty Eisner (Lattin, 2012, p. 198). Coincidently Eisner had written to Jung and said that for her LSD was "almost a religious drug" (Jung, 1984, p. 159). In August 1957, Jung replied to her and his letter encompasses his dislike of psychedelic drugs:

> Dear Mrs. Eisner:
>
> Thank you for your kind letter. Experiments along the line of mescaline and related drugs are certainly most interesting, since such drugs lay bare a level of the unconscious that is otherwise accessible only under peculiar psychic conditions ....
>
> I don't feel happy about these things, since you merely fall into such experiences without being able to integrate them ....
>
> To have so-called religious visions of this kind has more to do with physiology but nothing with religion. It is only that mental phenomena are observed which one can compare to similar images in ecstatic conditions.
>
> Religion is a way of life and a devotion and submission to certain superior facts—a state of mind which cannot be injected by a syringe or swallowed in the form of a pill.
>
> It is to my mind a helpful method to the barbarous Peyotee, but a regrettable regression for a cultivated individual, a dangerously simple "Ersatz" and substitute for a true religion.
>
> Sincerely yours,
> C. G. Jung (Jung, 1984, pp. 159–160)

John H. Laney (1972), in his dissertation *On the Scholarly Use of Jung's Writings*, is highly critical of Jung's stance, considering it to be "totally without substance" (Laney, p. 124). Laney writes that the smoking of Peyote is centred in a twelve-hour ceremony that is called a "prayer meeting" and is similar to the "Catholic High Mass", and Jung had therefore "vilified prayer, itself" (Laney, p. 125). Continuing, Laney wrote, "Jung's words are not distinguishable from those of the collective mentality which fantasizes the peyote meeting as a drug orgy, failing to realize that it is a prayer meeting" (Laney, p. 126).

CHAPTER TWO

Origins of A.A.: Bill Wilson's last drink and recovery

Serendipitous origins of A.A.: Ebby Thacher's visit to Bill Wilson,
and Bill's visit to Calvary Mission and Towns Hospital

As mentioned, Rowland Hazard was a patient of Carl Jung's in Kushnacht in Switzerland in 1926. Upon his return to America, Rowland followed Jung's advice, and joined an evangelical organisation called the Oxford Group. This group was based on a "simple religious idea and a practical program of action" (Anon, 2011, p. 9). Their religious principles included the "Four Absolutes" of Absolute Honesty, Absolute Unselfishness, Absolute Love, and Absolute Purity (Dick B., 1998, p. 31). After joining the Oxford Group, Rowland succeeded in stopping drinking—temporarily. In August 1934, Rowland heard that his friend, Edwin Thacher, nicknamed "Ebby", was about to be committed by a judge to an asylum in Vermont. Rowland and fellow members of the Oxford Group, Cebra Graves and Shep Cornell, decided to intervene and help Ebby. Rowland and Shep Cornell persuaded Judge Graves, who was the father of Cebra Graves, to "suspend" Ebby's commitment. Cebra and Shep then convinced Ebby to stop drinking and "lodged him in Calvary's mission over on the East side" of Manhattan where the Oxford groupers were holding meetings (Anon, 2000, p. 131). A few months later Ebby, following the Oxford Group guidelines, set out to pass his new found experience of sobriety onto Bill Wilson. It was "on a bleak November afternoon" when Ebby visited his "old school friend" and former drinking buddy, Bill Wilson, in the kitchen of his home on Clinton Street in Brooklyn (Anon, 2011, p. 36).

Wilson was born on 26 November 1895, which would have provided him with a good birthday excuse for drinking during November. Indeed, Wilson, who had been drinking that day, later wrote, "Of course he would have dinner, and then I could drink openly with him". Bill "pushed a drink across the table". Ebby refused the drink and "looked straight at me" and said, "simply, but smilingly … I've got religion" (Anon, 2011, p. 36). Bill, like many active alcoholics, was cynical about religion, but believed that Christ was, "a great man, not too closely followed by those who claimed him". However, his experiences in the First World War made him doubt "whether, on balance, the religions of mankind had done any good" (Ibid., p. 37).

That first afternoon in late November 1934, they spoke in Bill's basement kitchen "for hours" (Anon, 1991a, p. 10). Ebby rekindled in Bill a memory of when in 1917, as a US army officer, aged twenty-two he landed in England and visited Winchester Cathedral[1] where he was:

> much moved, I wandered outside. My attention was caught by doggerel on an old tombstone:
>
> > Here lies a Hampshire Grenadier.
> > Who caught his death
> > Drinking cold small beer.
> > A good soldier is ne'er forgot.
> > Whether he dieth by musket
> > Or by pot. (Anon, 1991a, p. 1)

Bill recalled this moment of clarity in the Winchester Cathedral graveyard as an "Ominous warning which I failed to heed" (Anon, 2011, p. 33). Bill remembered that during his talk with Ebby,

> The real significance of my experience in the cathedral burst upon me. For a brief moment, I had needed and wanted God. There had been a humble willingness to have Him with me—and He came.

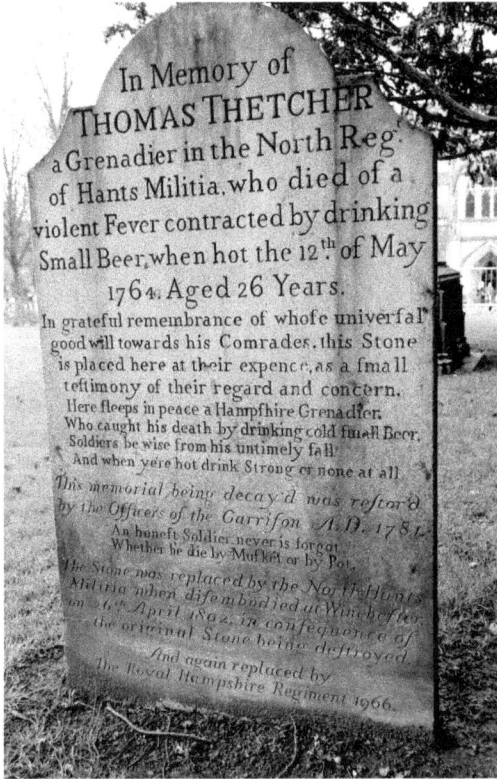

In Memory of
THOMAS THETCHER
a Grenadier in the North Reg.
of Hants Militia, who died of a
violent Fever contracted by drinking
Small Beer, when hot the 12.th of May
1764. Aged 26 Years.
In grateful remembrance of whose univerfal
good will towards his Comrades, this Stone
is placed here at their expence, as a fmall
teftimony of their regard and concern.
Here fleeps in peace a Hampfhire Grenadier,
Who caught his death by drinking cold fmall Beer,
Soldiers be wife from his untimely fall
And when ye're hot drink Strong or none at all
This memorial being decay'd was reftor'd
by the Officers of the Garrifon A.D. 1781.
An honeft Soldier never is forgot
Whether he die by Mufket or by Pot.
The Stone was replaced by the North Hants
Militia when difembodied at Winchefter
on 1.st April 1802, in confequence of
the original Stone being deftroyed
And again replaced by
the Royal Hampshire Regiment 1966.

Figure 1. Tombstone of Thomas Thetcher.

> But soon the sense of His presence had been blotted out by worldly
> clamours, mostly those within myself. And so it had been ever
> since. How blind I had been. (Anon, 2011, p. 38)

Coincidently the surname on the tombstone is Thetcher, and it is likely
that Bill was drawn to the tombstone because he wondered if it "could
be an ancestor" of his close friend Ebby Thacher (Anon, 1991b, p. 60).
Seventeen years later, Ebby Thacher became Bill's sponsor, taught him
about the principles of the Oxford Group and successfully planted the
idea of recovery in Bill's mind. According to Bill, during their talks
together they were engaged "in the kinship of common suffering, one
alcoholic talking to another" (Anon, 2005, p. 59). In particular, Ebby told
Bill, "that God had done for him what he could not do for himself."
Upon seeing this "miracle directly across the kitchen table," Bill began

to revise his ideas and thought that perhaps "religious people were right after all" (Anon, 2011, p. 37).

On 8 December 1934, Bill, enthused by Ebby's words set out to investigate the Oxford Group's headquarters, based in Calvary Mission at 346, East Twenty-third Street, Manhattan (Anon, 1979, p. 88). Travelling from Brooklyn by subway he "left the subway at Fourth Street heading to 23rd Street. It was a long walk across Twenty-Third, so I began stopping in bars. This consumed most of the afternoon, and I forgot all about the mission." He met a Finnish fisherman, Alec. "Somehow the word fisherman clicked. I thought again of the mission" (Anon, 2000, p. 136). Bill "stumbled into the Mission dragging Alec, the Finn, with him" (Anon, 1979, p. 88). The greeter on the door was about to refuse Bill entry, but Ebby Thacher spotted Bill, intervened, and welcomed him in. Ebby provided Bill and Alec the Finn with a snack of "coffee and some baked beans" (Ibid.). There was an evangelical service in progress. During the service the leader of the group called "for penitents to come forward" to offer themselves to God (Kurtz, 1991, p. 18). Bill's wife, Lois sets the scene graphically:

> Bill was greatly moved and started to do the same. Afraid he was still too drunk to be rational, Ebby grabbed his coattails, but to no avail. Bill marched to the front of the room and spoke as the others had. He also recounted a little of his fruitless search for permanent sobriety. He could never remember just what he said, but Ebby told us later that he made a very reasonable and moving speech. (Anon, 1979, p. 88)

Bill recalled that after the meeting,

> I saw the dormitories where the derelicts slept. I met a few who had made good recoveries ... Eagerly I listened to their stories. I sobered up very fast and the dead weight on me seemed to go on lifting ... Before going to bed, Lois and I had a long talk. There was hope in every word. Without an ounce of gin I slept like a child. (Anon, 2005, pp. 60–61)

Despite the good impression his visit to Calvary Mission had on him, the next evening "at six o'clock Lois found me upstairs on the bed dead drunk" (Anon, 2005, p. 61). Indeed for the next two days Bill "drank as he never had before" (Pittman, 1988, p. 152). Finally, on 11 December 1934, Bill decided to admit himself for his fourth detox to Towns Hospital at Central

Park West. Before leaving his home in Clinton Street he left a note for Lois on the kitchen table. It was written in pencil and told of his hope for recovery and poignantly and tenderly expressed his everlasting love to Lois. Lois's response to that note was one of anger and frustration: It is worth quoting this paragraph in full because it shows the need for Al-Anon!

> Bill had left a note for me at home. Upon finding it I was quite upset. Why hadn't he consulted me about going to the hospital? What good would it do anyway? He would get drunk again the minute he left. Who was going to pay the bill? The money I earned was just barely enough to keep us going—including Bill's liquor bills. We had been forced to ask for help in the payment of the previous hospital bills, but we couldn't do it again. Dad had no money. Where could I get it? We had occasionally pawned some silver; perhaps I could sell some wedding presents now. But what possible permanent good could it do for Bill to go to the hospital again? (Anon, 1979, p. 89)

Having written the note to Lois, Bill walked to the subway. According to his memoir he "fished six cents out of my pocket. Never mind, I thought, a nickel would get me to the hospital". Bill decided, "I might as well be comfortable until the hospital took over". Although he was in debt at the grocery store he explained his plight and acquired four bottles of beer "on the cuff" and drank them on the street and on the subway to the hospital (Anon, 2000, p. 140). He was admitted at 2:30 p.m. and he showed signs of delirium tremens (Anon, 1991a, p. 13). While in Towns Hospital he was treated with a number of sedatives, including Belladonna, which, according to his biographer, Susan Cheevers, can induce hallucinations (Cheever, 2004, p. 114).

Bill Wilson's spiritual experience in Towns Hospital

Ebby visited Bill in Towns Hospital and repeated the Oxford Group's principles to Bill. One day after Ebby left, Bill wrote that;

> my depression deepened unbearably and finally it seemed to me as though I were at the bottom of the pit. I still gagged badly on the notion of a Power greater than myself, but finally, just for the moment the last vestige of my proud obstinacy was crushed. All at once I found myself crying out, 'If there be a God, let Him show

Himself! I am ready to do anything, anything!' Suddenly the room lit up with a great white light. I was caught up into an ecstasy which there are no words to describe. It seemed to me, in my mind's eye, that I was on a mountain and that a wind not of air but of spirit was blowing. And then it burst upon me that I was a free man. (Anon, 2005, p. 63)

For a moment Bill was "alarmed" and asked the doctor in charge at the Hospital, Dr. Silkwood, if he was still sane. Fortunately Silkwood did not sedate him and instead wisely told him, "Something has happened to you I don't understand. But you had better hang on to it. Anything is better than the way you were" (Anon, 1991a, p. 14).

Bill Wilson never had another drink after that spiritual experience. Many religious and mystical traditions see religious experiences as revelations caused by divine agency rather than ordinary natural processes. They are considered real encounters with God or gods, or real contact with higher-order realities of which humans are not ordinarily aware ("Religious experience", 2014).

Soon after his "mystical" experience, Ebby brought Bill a copy of William James's *The Varieties of Religious Experience*. This book provided Bill with "the realization that most conversion experiences, whatever their variety, do have a common denominator of ego collapse at depth". Bill recorded in his letter to Jung that his "release from the alcohol obsession was immediate. At once I knew I was a free man" (see Appendix One).

Shortly after his spiritual experience, Lois visited Bill in Towns Hospital. Despite her earlier scepticism when reading the note he left, she later wrote:

> The minute I saw him at the hospital, I knew something overwhelming had happened. His eyes were filled with light. His whole being expressed hope and joy. From that moment on I shared his confidence in the future. I never doubted that at last he was free. I walked home on air. (Anon, 1979, p. 89)

Following his spiritual experience Bill wrote:

> I humbly offered myself to God, as I then understood Him, to do with me as He would. I placed myself unreservedly under His care and direction. I admitted for the first time that of myself I was nothing; that without Him I was lost. I ruthlessly faced my sins and was

willing to have my new found Friend take them away, root and branch. I have not had a drink since. (Anon, 2011, p. 38)

Bill later wrote about his meetings with Ebby in Towns Hospital. The talk is worth quoting because in this short paragraph several of the twelve steps are covered:

> My school mate visited me, and I fully acquainted him with my problems and deficiencies. We made a list of people I had hurt or toward whom I felt resentment. I expressed an entire willingness to approach these individuals, admitting my wrong. (Ibid.)

Bill thought that these principles seemed, "Simple, but not easy, a price had to be paid. It meant destruction of self-centeredness. I must turn in all things to the Father of Light who presides over us all" (Ibid.). Ebby told Bill that it was, "essential to work with others, as he had worked with me" (Anon, 2011, p. 39). This was the genesis of Alcoholics Anonymous.

According to Bill:

> While I lay in the hospital, the thought came that there were thousands of hopeless alcoholics who might be glad to have what had been so freely given me. Perhaps I could help some of them. They in turn might work with others. (Anon, 1991a, p. 14)

Bill was excited by the idea and his "thoughts began to race as I envisioned a chain reaction among alcoholics, one carrying this message and these principles to the next. More than I could ever want anything else, I now knew that I wanted to work with other alcoholics" (Anon, 2005, p. 64). Following his discharge from Towns Hospital in January 1935, Bill Wilson, aged thirty-nine, joined the Oxford Group and never drank alcohol again. He began to try and help other alcoholics by telling them about his own recovery. Lois supported him in his vision and together they dedicated themselves "with enthusiasm to the idea of helping other alcoholics to a solution of their problem" (Anon, 2011, p. 39).

> My wife and I abandoned ourselves with enthusiasm to the idea of helping other alcoholics to a solution of their problem. It was

fortunate, for my old business associates remained skeptical for a year and a half, during which I found little work. I was not too well at the time, and was plagued by waves of self-pity and resentment. This sometimes nearly drove me back to drink. I soon found that when all other measures failed, work with another alcoholic would save the day. Many times I have gone to my old hospital in despair. On talking to a man there, I would be amazingly lifted up and set on my feet. (Ibid.)

Bill introduced alcoholics to the Oxford Group. Despite his enthusiasm Bill was not having much success helping alcoholics to remain sober. However, he became aware that this work at least was helping him to remain sober.

A Jungian interpretation of a spiritual experience

In the Big Book, *Alcoholics Anonymous*, Bill Wilson quoted Jung's description of a spiritual experience as he told it to Rowland Hazard:

> Once in a while alcoholics have had what are called vital spiritual experiences. To me these occurrences are phenomena. They appear to be in the nature of huge emotional displacements and rear-rangements. Ideas, emotions, and attitudes which were once the guiding forces of these men are suddenly cast to one side, and a completely new set of conceptions and motives begin to dominate them. (Anon, 1991a, p. 27)

Bill Wilson understood exactly what Jung meant as he himself had such a dramatic spiritual experience in Towns Hospital in December 1934.

Spiritual experiences and spiritual awakenings are terms that are used interchangeably in A.A.[2] However, more people may be having spiritual experiences than they admit. The main reason I was prompted to write about alcoholism was because of the stories people in recovery were telling me about hearing voices that came from outside of them-selves. Their stories were remarkably similar.

In particular, one recovering alcoholic told me that while taking care of his young daughter on a Sunday afternoon he realised that:

I felt nothing for her which petrified me, so I picked her up and sent her to her mother's house. That night I went to bed drunk and woke up around three in the morning and made a very clear decision that I was going to the gun cabinet in my cupboard and was going up to the park, to the part where there is hidden rough ground and I was going to commit suicide. As I was lifting my legs off the bed to go and put them down on the floor, a very small quiet confident commanding voice said, "Stay in bed, don't do this" and I decided I was going to ignore that voice and carry on. I went to move my feet again and it repeated in exactly the same tone, at exactly the same level, the exact same command, "Stay in bed and ask for help in the morning". The voice was outside me and inside me at the same time, which sounds bizarre. (personal communication from A.A. member, 24 August 2014)

Hearing these stories about "voices" made me realise that these voices were not "schizophrenic" or pathological in any way. I realised that there was another feature to addiction. It is the spiritual aspect. Jungian psychology is one of the few psychological theories that recognise the importance of the spiritual dimension of men and women.

In his clinical writings Jung described two occurrences, albeit not alcoholics, that are similar to Bill Wilson's spiritual experience.

The first incident was that of a patient who had progressive paralysis and wanted to kill himself; just as he was about to jump from the windowsill, "a tremendous light appeared in front of the window, hurling him back into the room" (CW 3, para. 305).

The second case was that of a "psychopath" who was so sickened by his life that he decided to kill himself by inhaling gas. However, he:

suddenly felt an enormous hand grasp him by the chest and throw him to the floor, where he gradually recovered from his fright. The hallucination was so distinct that the next day he could still show me the place where the five fingers had gripped him. (CW 3, para. 306)

From a Jungian perspective, the above experiences are a metaphor for the death of the ego, which allows the true Self to be heard. The case of the psychopath is more relevant to A.A. as it has a strong element of a person seeking repentance. Effectively, in the case of the "psychopath", the kinesthetic energy that created the hallucinatory hand allowed the body to remain alive so that the true Self could continue to live through the person. According to Jung this energy is beyond personal control because it does not come from the ego:

> It is as though, at the climax of the illness, the destructive powers were converted into healing forces .... As a religious-minded person would say: guidance has come from God. ... To the patient it is nothing less than a revelation when something altogether strange rises up to confront him from the hidden depths of the psyche—something that is not his ego and is therefore beyond the reach of his personal will. He has regained access to the sources of psychic life, and this marks the beginning of the cure. (CW 11, para. 534)

Jung understands why these experiences then bring sobriety:

> Such experiences reward the sufferer for the pains of the labyrinthine way. From now on a light shines through the confusion; more, he can accept the conflict within him and so come to resolve the morbid split in his nature on a higher level. (CW 11, para. 536)

One explanation for hearing an external voice is that in times of crisis there may be an independent psychic energy that can emanate from the true Self and override the ego in order to protect the Self. It's as though the true Self can act to protect itself from suicidal annihilation by the ego and shows itself by acting or speaking out. Once the true Self emerges then the ego seems to know its lesser place from then on. The person's ego begins to slowly learn that there is a power greater that it and that the ego is subservient to this Higher Power. Conventional psychiatry can offer no explanation for such "voices", and instead we might remember the wisdom of Shakespeare who said "There are more things in heaven and earth, Horatio, than are dreamt of in your philosophy" (Shakespeare, 1958, 1.5.167–8).

The hearing of a voice outside of oneself is not necessarily pathological. It may be the true Self in survival mode speaking and being heard by the ego. After all, when the ego decides to suicide, it brings the true Self with it as well.

The experiences can be called moments of clarity. One such moment led to Bill reaching out to another alcoholic resulting in the formation of A.A.

Bill Wilson visits Akron and meets Dr. Bob

In May 1935, Bill decided to engage in some work related to his defunct career in stock broking. This entailed a visit to Akron, Ohio (Anon, 2005, p. 65). Bill visited Akron to organise a shareholders takeover of a company involved in the manufacture of rubber products. The company is today called the National Rubber Machinery Company and it is still in existence. The idea was that the shareholders he represented would take control of the company and manage it to greater profitability so that its stock price would rise. The shareholders Bill represented were outvoted by the majority of other shareholders and the trip was a financial failure. He felt, "bitterly discouraged" (Anon, 2011, p. 103).

He was almost broke and realised that he was in a precarious situation and considered drinking. It was the eve of Mother's Day. This may have reminded him that shortly after his parents' divorce, at the age of ten, he was abandoned first by his father and then by his mother who left him to be reared by his grandparents (Cheever, 2004, p. 21). Bill was tempted by the gaiety coming from the hotel bar. He "wanted to talk with someone, but whom?" (Anon, 2011, p. 103). Bill paced up and down the lobby of the Mayflower Hotel in Akron. He was in the grip of what is sometimes described as being in a state of two minds, a battle between the primitive reptile brain (unconscious) and the new frontal cortex brain of humans (conscious); perhaps more simply a struggle between the damaged ego and the true Self. Bill recorded that moment in the third person: It is worth citing in full because it may be the most pivotal moment in the formation of A.A.

> At one end of the room stood a glass covered directory of local churches. Down the lobby a door opened into an attractive bar. He could see the gay crowd inside. In there he would find companionship and release. Unless he took some drinks, he might not have the courage to scrape an acquaintance, and would have a lonely week-end.

Of course, he couldn't drink, but why not sit hopefully at a table, a bottle of ginger ale before him? Then after all, had he not been sober six months now? Perhaps he could handle, say three drinks—no more! Fear gripped him. He was on thin ice. Again it was the old, insidious insanity—that first drink. With a shiver, he turned away and walked down the lobby to the church directory. Music and gay chatter still floated to him from the bar. But what about his responsibilities . . . and yes those other alcoholics? There must be many of them in this town. He would phone a clergyman. His sanity returned, and he thanked God. Selecting a church at random from the directory, he stepped into a booth and lifted the receiver. (Anon, 2011, p. 103)

He eventually connected to an Episcopalian Minister, Walter Tunks, who coincidentally was a member of the Oxford Group. Bill explained his predicament of needing to talk to another alcoholic (Kurtz, 1991, p. 27). Tunks gave him the phone numbers of ten people the last of whom, Norman Shepherd referred him to Mrs. Henrietta Seiberling (Ibid.). Bill recognised the Seiberling name and her connection to the

Figure 2. Picture of Bill Wilson in the foyer of the Mayflower Hotel.

company tycoon who owned Goodyear Tyre Company, which was linked to the recent business dealings he had failed in.

If he were to describe himself to a member of the Sieberling family as an alcoholic it would be further humiliation. However, Bill went to his room and it was from there he eventually decided to make the call to Henrietta Seiberling. This was probably his twelfth phone call. Bill recalled that "Of the ten people to whom I had been directed by Clergyman Walter Tunks, Henrietta was the only one who had understood enough and cared enough" (Anon, 2005, p. 73). Henrietta was estranged from her husband, who was the son of the Goodyear tyre tycoon. She lived in a modest gate lodge at the entrance to the huge family estate. Henrietta was also a member of the Oxford Group and knew that fellow member of the Oxford Group, Dr. Bob Smith, had a chronic drink problem. Henrietta later recalled that due to her concern for Dr. Bob, Bill's phone call was "really manna from heaven" (Anon, 1991b, p. 137). Henrietta arranged a dinner meeting for Bill at 5 p.m., the next day with Dr. Bob Smith and his wife Anne. Reputedly, Dr. Bob was "passed out under his dining-room table" when Henrietta Seiberling phoned (Kurtz, 1991, p. 28). Bob's wife, Anne, managed to get him to agree to meet Bill for fifteen minutes in Henrietta's gatehouse the next evening (Ibid.). There must have been great trust in the air given that a stranger who was a self-confessed alcoholic was asking to meet a surgeon and offer him help!

When they first met Dr. Bob was "twitching and trembling" from a severe hangover, however, he and Bill ended up talking for over seven hours. During this time, they shared their experiences of alcoholism and difficulties remaining sober (Ibid.). Bill and Dr. Bob became friends and continued to talk with each other about their common problem of alcoholism.

According to Bill, "Three or four weeks after their first meeting Dr. Bob then went to a medical convention in Atlantic City" (Anon, 2005, p. 70). Nothing was heard from Dr. Bob for a week. In fact he "went on a roaring bender", and for him this was the spree that ended all sprees (Anon, 2011, p. 104). That was reputedly on 10 June 1935, when Bill and Bob began their "outreach" work in Akron City Hospital. That date is recognised as the official founding date of Alcoholics Anonymous. However, in the General Service Office, New York, there is a picture of Dr. Bob with his colleagues at that convention, dated 17 June. Given that Dr. Bob drank during and after the conference, it is logical that Dr. Bob had his last drink after he returned to Akron, which was after 17 June 1935. Kurtz (1991) notes that while Bill thought it was 10 June; it was more likely, 28 June 1935 (p. 322, fn 22).

Bill and Bob's "12 step" calling began at the end of June 1935, when Dr. Bob phoned the head nurse at Akron City Hospital and "inquired if she had a first class alcoholic prospect" (Anon, 2011, p. 104). The nurse knew Dr. Bob and of his drinking. She told him that there was a "real corker" in the hospital who had begun his detox by "physically assaulting two nurses" (Kurtz, 1991, p. 37). Two days later Bill and Bob called on the "prospect" in the hospital. He was a lawyer and former city councilman and church deacon (Anon, 2011, pp. 104–105). They spoke to him as equals and shared their experiences of alcoholism and spoke about how their spiritual experience helped keep them sober. After listening to Bill and Bob, "the prospect" told them his story:

> No, I'm too far gone for that. I've always believed in God. I used to be a deacon in the church. But, boys, I've been in and out of this place six times in the last four months. This time in d.t.'s I badly beat up one of the nurses. I know I can't even get home from here sober. I'm afraid to go out. No, it's too late for me. I still believe in God alright, but I know mighty well that He doesn't believe in me anymore. (Anon, 2005, p. 72)

Bill and Bob persisted and again visited him the next day. "On the third day the lawyer gave his life to the care and direction of his Creator, and said he was perfectly willing to do anything necessary". He never drank again (Anon, 2011, p. 105). His name was Bill Dobbs and he is recognised as the third person to get sober in A.A.

Bill continued to work with alcoholics in New York under the auspices of the Oxford Group. However, Bill was criticised by a "young associate" Oxford Group pastor for forming a "secret ashamed sub-group" engaged in "divergent work" (Kurtz, 1991, p. 45). Bill learned that alcoholics from the Oxford Group were banned from attending meetings in his home in Clinton Street. According to Bill "The Oxford Group wanted to save the world, and I only wanted to save drunks" (Kurtz, 1991, p. 322, fn 22). In 1937, Bill split with the Oxford Group and, together with Dr. Bob, formed their own group, which became known as Alcoholics Anonymous. Later Bill, supported by Dr. Bob, decided that a book explaining how A.A. works should be written (Anon, 2012, p. 123).

Bill Wilson writes the "Big Book"—Alcoholics Anonymous

In December 1938, Bill started writing a book to explain how his work with alcoholics meeting in groups was keeping them sober. He began by asking recovering alcoholics to send their stories to him for consideration for inclusion in the forthcoming book popularly called the Big Book. This is the "Bible" of A.A. and explains the steps, how the programme works, and includes advice on relations with family and employers. It also contains the stories of recovering alcoholics who remain sober through working the twelve steps of A.A. Bill sent drafts of the chapters around to the groups for their comments.

One of the major controversies concerned the usage of the term "God" in the twelve steps. While the term remained in steps three and eleven, the codicil was added that it was "a God of one's own understanding". This was accepted by atheists and agnostics and contributed to opening the door of A.A. to many alcoholics to whom the term "God" had unacceptable dogmatic religious overtones. Ironically, while step three does say "God as we understood Him", it does presumptuously assume the outmoded patriarchal term.

Over a hundred titles were considered including *Dry Frontiers*, *The Empty Glass*, and *The Way Out* (Anon, 2005, p. 166). However, there were already several books with the latter title. The New York group had called themselves a "nameless bunch of drunks". A member of the nameless bunch, a former writer for the *New Yorker*, came up with the name "Alcoholics Anonymous" (Anon, 1979, pp. 114–115). This title suited Wilson as it signalled to him not to claim authorship publicly. He admitted that he had "in one dark moment" forgotten that "this was everybody's book" and considered naming it "The B.W. Movement", but more modestly realised that he was "mostly the umpire of the discussions" (Anon, 2005, p. 165). While the title of the book is *Alcoholics Anonymous*, it is popularly referred to as the "Big Book". It was from the title of the book Alcoholics Anonymous that the name of the organisation was derived.

According to Dr. Bob he "had nothing to do with the writing" (cited in Kurtz, 1991, p. 331, fn 31). However, Bill did spend three months living in Dr. Bob's family home in Akron, where Bill and Bob stayed up most nights talking and drinking coffee until the early hours of the morning. According to Dr. Bob, "It would be hard for me to conceive that something wasn't said at or during these nightly discussions around our kitchen table that influenced the actual writing of the Twelve Steps" (Ibid.).

Kurtz gives a graphic account of Bill's first attempts to start writing:

> Sprawling on his bed in an anything but a spiritual mood one evening, Wilson poised his yellow pencil over the school tablet propped before him. Quickly, lest he block, he scrawled the words "How It Works" across the top of the page. (Kurtz, 1991, p. 69)

He then wrote out six stories that were based on what he had learned at the Oxford Group, but considered it "too preachy" (Ibid.). Wilson was in a dilemma; New York alcoholics found the Oxford Group's four absolutes—absolute honesty, absolute purity, absolute unselfishness, and absolute love—"too rich". However, Akron A.A., which had retained the Oxford Group absolutes, was having more success in retaining members. So Wilson had to write something that would be agreeable to both New York and Akron. Further, "There must not be a single loophole through which the rationalizing alcoholic could wiggle out". According to Bill, he,

> Relaxed and asked for guidance. With a speed that was astonishing, considering my jangling emotions, I completed the first draft. It took perhaps half an hour. The words kept right on coming. When I reached a stopping point, I numbered the new steps. They added up to twelve. Somehow this number seemed significant. Without any special rhyme or reason I connected them with the twelve apostles. (Anon, 2005, p. 161)

Kurtz has reconstructed how the twelve steps were written that evening: "Bill's pencil then began to fly over the paper, and his thoughts continued to flow" as he wrote a paragraph beginning:

> Half measures will avail you nothing. You stand at the turning point. Throw yourself under God's protection and care with complete abandon.
>
> Now we think you can take it! Here are the steps we took—our program of recovery. (Kurtz, 1991, p. 70)

The twelve steps as written that evening are the same that are in use today except for a few minor modifications. For example: In step three Bill originally wrote "Made a decision to turn our wills and our lives over to the care of God" (Ibid.). However, reputedly at the behest of an agnostic member, "as we understood him" was added (see also Dick, 1997, p. 64).

Step eight was originally written by Bill as "Humbly on our knees asked Him to remove our shortcomings" (Kurtz, 1991, p. 70). This was subsequently changed to read "Humbly asked Him to remove our shortcomings".

Step eleven originally read, "Sought through prayer and meditation to improve our conscious contact with God, praying only for knowledge of His will for us and the power to carry that out" (Ibid.). However, as in step three the concerns of members who were agnostic or atheist were catered for and the words "as we understood Him" were inserted into step eleven so today the step reads: "Sought through prayer and meditation to improve our conscious contact with God as we understood Him, praying only for knowledge of His will for us and the power to carry that out."

"Almost idly," he began to number the new steps (Ibid.). According to his wife Lois, "when he finished writing and reread what he had put down, he was quite pleased. Twelve principles had developed—the Twelve Steps" (Anon, 1979, p. 113).

Wilson readily admitted that he based his twelve steps on the knowledge and principles learned from the Oxford Group. Referring to the Episcopal clergyman, Sam Shoemaker, the former leader of the Oxford Group in America, Wilson wrote,

> that many a channel had been used by Providence to create Alcoholics Anonymous. … But the important thing is this: the early A.A. had got its ideas of self-examination, acknowledgement of character defects, restitution for harm done, and working with others straight from the Oxford Groups and directly from Sam Shoemaker, their former leader in America, and from nowhere else. (Anon, 2005, p. 39)

There seems to be less emphasis on the connection between the programme of A.A. and Christianity. However, Dick B. (one of the doyens of the history of Alcoholics Anonymous) has written a detailed analysis of the connection between the Bible and the Big Book in *The Good Book and The Big Book: A.A.'s Roots in the Bible* (1997).

In 1938, Bill's home in Clinton Street, which he had inherited from his father-in-law, was repossessed. He was in a precarious financial position and had to rely on friends to accommodate Lois and himself. Still Bill set about finding the finances for printing the Big Book. Firstly there was an attempt to raise the money from fellow alcoholics by issuing shares in the "Works Publishing, Inc." (Anon, 2005, p. 157). Initially no money was raised, and then Charles B. Towns, proprietor of the detox hospital Bill recovered in, offered $2,500 towards the publication costs (Ibid., p. 159).

Initially there was little uptake of the Big Book. The Big Book was so called because initially the first edition was printed on thick paper. Despite sending out 20,000 postcards with order forms to physicians they only received two genuine orders (Anon, 2005, pp. 175–176).

An article about A.A. was carried by *Liberty* magazine in the Fall of 1939, resulting in some 800 urgent calls to their office for help. Each enquiry received a personal letter and a small pamphlet. Attention was also drawn to the book *Alcoholics Anonymous*, which soon moved into brisk circulation. Aided by mail from New York, and by A.A. travellers from already established centres, many new groups were created. At the end of 1939, the membership of A.A. stood at 2,000.

In March 1941, Jack Alexander, a lead writer with the *Saturday Evening Post*, wrote a well-researched article about A.A.; the response overwhelmed the small A.A. office. By the close of that year, membership of A.A. had jumped to 6,000, and the number of groups multiplied in proportion.

An International Convention was held in St. Louis in 1955 to celebrate the Fellowship's twentieth anniversary. Here, Bill turned the future care and custody of A.A. over to the conference and its trustees. By this time, the fellowship of A.A. had matured and was psychologically independent of its founder.

It was on 24 January 1971, that Bill, a victim of pneumonia, died in Miami Beach, Florida. His biographer, Susan Cheever, records that on Christmas day, 1970, while delirious on his death bed he asked for "three shots of whiskey" and also in early January 1971, for a single shot of whiskey (Cheever, 2004, p. 248). Charitably, it may be assumed that Bill, who had not taken an alcoholic drink for over thirty-six years, was in his death throes and his delirious requests for whiskey should not be taken too seriously in the face of his overall commitment to abstinence and sobriety. Instead it should be remembered that Sotheby's, when auctioning the original manuscript of the Big Book, described it as "one of the most influential books of the twentieth century" (Anon, 2011, preface, p. 16). In 1999, *Time* magazine nominated Bill Wilson as one of "Time's 100 persons of the century" (Ibid.).

The next chapter will attempt to understand alcoholism from a medical, and psychological perspective using case notes of a male and female alcoholic whom Jung treated.

CHAPTER THREE

Understanding alcoholism from a medical perspective and through the writings of Carl Jung

Medical and psychological attempts to diagnose alcoholism

There is no medical definition of the term alcoholic. A Swedish physician, Magnus Huss reputedly first coined the word alcoholism in a book titled *Alcoholismus Chronicus* [Chronic Alcoholism] (Blocker, 2003, p. 61).

There is an adage that if the patient with an alcohol problem does not drink as much as their doctor then they cannot be an alcoholic. When subjected to duress, an alcoholic may consult their family physician but usually takes care to be sober and on his or her very best behaviour. The patient then usually under-reports the volume of consumption of alcohol. They may be told by their doctor to "cut down" and may be prescribed a low dose of tranquilisers to cope with the stress of work, family relationships, etc. This consultation, while it may provide short-term relief for the alcoholic, it is usually a disaster for them in the long term. It simply postpones the day of reckoning and endangers the life of the alcoholic and means the "rock bottom" may have to get even lower. Possibly, the most reliable person to diagnose alcoholism is the local "street gossip".

The medical and psychological communities have tried in vain to define alcoholism. In 1990, a twenty-three member committee of the combined National Council on Alcoholism and the American Society of Addiction Medicine combined to provide a definition of alcoholism. The goals of the committee were to create a definition that was scientifically valid, clinically useful, and understandable by the general public. After two years the committee agreed to define alcoholism as:

> A primary, chronic disease with genetic, psychosocial, and environmental factors influencing its development and manifestations. The disease is often progressive and fatal. It is characterized by continuous or periodic impaired control over drinking, preoccupation with the drug alcohol, use of alcohol despite adverse consequences, and distortions in thinking, most notably denial. (Morse & Flavin, 1992, p. 1012)

In 2013 the American Psychiatric Association published the fifth *Diagnostic and Statistical Manual of Mental Disorders* (DSM-5). The manual provides detailed lists of symptoms of mental disorders. This version of the DSM decided to disregard the previous distinction between alcohol abuse and alcohol dependence that was in the DSM-IV. This was because the distinction between alcohol abuse and alcohol dependence caused confusion over the subtle distinctions. Instead the current DSM-5 now uses the term alcohol disorder.

The DSM-5 (pp. 490–491) lists eleven criteria for the diagnosis of alcohol disorder, these include:

1. Drinking alcohol in larger amounts or for longer than intended
2. Unsuccessful efforts to cut down or stop using alcohol
3. Spending a lot of time drinking or recovering
4. Craving or strong desire to drink
5. Not fulfilling major obligations due to recurrent drinking
6. Continuing to drink, despite the legal, social and family consequences
7. Giving priority to drinking over important social, occupational or recreational activities
8. Continuing to drink despite health warnings
9. Continuing to drink even though it is causing or exacerbating physical or psychological problems

10. Having to drink more in order to get the same effect as before (tolerance)
11. Experiencing withdrawal symptoms and taking substances such as tranquillisers to relieve or avoid the symptoms. (American Psychiatric Association, DSM-5, 2013, pp. 490–491)

Possibly the most practical diagnostic screening aid for determining whether a person may be alcoholic is the CAGE questionnaire. This short questionnaire is a widely-used assessment instrument for screening tendencies towards alcoholism. The acronym helps any counsellor, physician, psychologist, or psychiatrist memorise four simple questions without resorting to a lengthy questionnaire.

These four questions are:

1. Have you ever tried to Cut down on your drinking?
2. Have you been Annoyed by people being critical of your drinking?
3. Have you ever felt Guilty about your drinking?
4. Have you ever had a drink first thing in the morning (Eye-opener) to steady your nerves or to get rid of a hangover?

Two "yes" responses indicate that the possibility of alcoholism should be investigated further. In my experience people rarely answer yes to needing to drink first thing in the morning. However, they will admit in a macho manner to "having the hair of the dog". Possibly another question that could be added is: Have you ever had a blackout? A positive response to this question is an indication that dangerous and damaging amounts of alcohol are being consumed.

Understanding alcoholism through the case histories of C. G. Jung: a male alcoholic

Jung's personal acquaintance with the effects and consequences of over-indulgence with alcohol began when he was fourteen. The family doctor advised his parents that he be sent on a holiday "for a cure". Jung does not say from what. While on the holiday Jung visited a distillery to "sample the wares". Jung described an ecstatic experience:

> I found the various little glasses so inspiring that I was wafted into a new and unexpected state of consciousness. There was no longer any inside or outside, no longer an "I" and the "others," No. 1 and

No. 2 were no more; caution and timidity were gone, and the earth and sky, the universe and everything in it that creeps and flies, revolves, rises, or falls, had all become one. I was shamefully, gloriously, triumphantly drunk. It was as if I were drowned in a sea of blissful musings, but, because of the violent heaving of the waves, had to cling with eyes, hands, and feet to all solid objects in order to keep my balance on the swaying streets and between the rocking houses and trees. "Marvellous", I thought, "only unfortunately just a little too much." The experience came to a rather woeful end, but it nevertheless remained a discovery, a premonition of beauty and meaning which I had spoiled only by my stupidity. (*Memories, Dreams, Reflections*, p. 96)

While Jung did not elaborate on his "woeful end", his story will resonate with many alcoholics' memory of their first experience of drinking alcohol to excess. As a university student, Jung had a reputation as a drinker and was nicknamed "the barrel". He was "known to his old school and drinking companions as a very merry member of the Zofingia[1] student club", and though "rarely drunk, but when so, was noisy" (Jaffe, 1970, pp. 22–23).

After gaining his medical degree in 1900, Jung began working at the psychiatric hospital of the University of Zurich, popularly called "the Burghölzli". The director of the hospital was Eugene Bleuler. Some of his patients were chronic alcoholics. His predecessor Auguste-Henri Forel attempted to treat alcoholic patients with a social drinking regime, serving them wine with lunch and dinner. This is now referred to as "controlled drinking". He found it was a disastrous failure and then on the advice of the local shoemaker who was a teetotaler, instituted a policy of alcohol abstinence for all patients and staff. His successor Bleuler, continued this policy and insisted that all staff should abstain from alcohol as role models for the patients (Brewer, pp. 4–5). Jung was dedicated to his work and abided by this edict while working there. Freud was critical of Forel, and in 1908 he taunted Jung about his abstinence from alcohol as being due to Forel's original edict banning alcohol and added "I won't say much about the most recent wave of abuse. Forel's attacks are chiefly on you" (Freud/Jung Letters, 1979, p. 126). In a sycophantic response to Freud, Jung called Forel a "hair shirt John of the locusts" and resumed drinking alcohol again (Ibid., p. 176). Fifty years later Jung was questioned about his comments on

Forel's policy on alcohol abstinence. He described his earlier remarks to Freud as an,

> inexpungerable reminder of the incredible folly that filled the days of my youth. The journey from cloud-cuckoo-land back to reality lasted a long time. (Brewer, 1987, pp. 4–5)

After reading Jung's report of his own immature drunken state and his perceptive and strikingly realistic descriptions of his alcoholic patients' mental states and their behaviours, it may be best to allow Jung to inform us about the varied symptoms and actions to be expected from alcoholics in full bloom. Jung recorded that in four years, between 1900 and 1904, 1,325 patients were admitted to the Burghölzli. Remarkably, only twenty were recorded as "being due to alcohol" (CW 3, para. 328).

Therefore, Jung would have overseen the treatment of an average of five alcoholic patients each year. From the examples he gives it appears that for the diagnosis of alcoholism or "degeneracy" as he occasionally referred to it, the patients had to be at the extreme end of the alcoholic spectrum. It is likely that he also treated many more patients who experienced general alcohol dependence but who presented with other psychological symptoms.

In his professional capacity, Jung was interested in the illness of alcoholism and began compiling notes on cases involving alcohol "degeneracy". The details of his patients' abuse of alcohol illustrate the commonality of the illness of alcoholism in mental hospitals then and arguably, now. Jung's work with patients who had alcohol problems allowed him to develop a specific list of symptoms related to alcohol dependency. Interestingly, he did not always view the alcohol problem as a primary illness whereas today, in terms of mental illness, alcoholism is diagnosed as a primary illness which means that most other psychological symptoms take a secondary role to alcoholism. If alcoholism forms part of a dual diagnosis it is advisable to have the person stop drinking so the secondary illness can be diagnosed independently of the influence of alcohol.

Jung wrote insightfully of the effects of alcohol abuse as leading to "over-accentuation of the ego, periodicity of various symptoms, such as irritability, depression, exacerbation of stable abnormalities, hysterical traits etc., found in nearly all cases of degeneracy" (CW 1, para. 191). The effects of alcoholism that he outlines have not changed and could make a valuable addition to the list of behavioural and emotional symptoms associated with alcoholism today. Jung understood the compulsiveness involved in alcoholism and indeed all addictions:

> For compulsion is the great mystery of human life. It is the thwarting of our conscious will and of our reason by an inflammable element within us, appearing now as a consuming fire and now as life-giving warmth. (CW 14, para. 1517)

In the first example, Jung illustrates the case of a young man, aged twenty-six who was a chronic alcoholic and is described as a "business man" (CW 1, para. 193).

His graphic account of the emotions and actions of this young man serve as a classic case study. It would also interest members of Al-Anon because it illustrates many of the symptoms and behavioural idiosyncrasies that people living with active alcoholics experience. The young man was admitted voluntarily to the Burghölzli in 1901. It was noted that on admission he was "slightly inebriated, euphoric, very talkative, showing flights of ideas" (CW 1, para. 194).

Many people with alcohol problems when entering rehabilitation have one last drink. For example on 11 December 1934, Bill Wilson, remembers that he managed to get four bottles of beer "on the cuff" from his local grocery store. He drank three of them along the way to his final detox in Towns Hospital: "Holding the last bottle by the neck, I walked into Towns where Dr. Silkworth met me in the hall" (Anon, 2005, p. 62).

Jung's patient told him that when not drinking he would become so irritated with his mother and sister that,

> He had to keep a grip on himself to prevent himself from banging both fists on the table. He couldn't settle down to any work, a "terrible inner restlessness" plagued him continually, an "everlasting restless urge to get away" to change his situation, kept him from any profitable activity. (CW 1, para. 193)

According to Jung, the illness displayed by this young man "was certainly not a case of simple alcoholism, since the psychic abnormality persisted even during abstinence" (CW 1, para. 195).

Jung may not have known that it takes approximately six weeks for alcohol to leave the body. Symptoms of withdrawal persist in what Terry Gorski, an expert on relapse prevention, refers to as the post-acute withdrawal period. According to Gorski, during these six weeks many symptoms such as sleeplessness, tremors, and mental confusion may continue (Gorski, 1989, pp. 34–35). Alcoholics in withdrawal are actually living out a mental torment called "white knuckling" or being in a state called "dry drunk". So, while not drinking they are in effect displaying many of the character defects normally associated with being drunk or severely hung over, such as anger and being in an agitated state.

Jung also described the symptoms of this young man as "manic" and "psychopathic". Many alcoholics suffer with depression, and indeed alcohol can be a form of self-medication. The corollary is that alcohol is a depressant which eventually leads to evident symptoms of depression. It is possible that Jung's patient had combined dual diagnosis of alcoholism and Bipolar depression and his alcoholism was masking his depression.

Jung continues his report on this man:

> He chased one pleasure after another and consumed enormous quantities of alcohol. His relatives finally decided to yield to his cravings, change and let him go abroad, where he obtained a position in a branch of the firm. But things didn't work out there either. (CW 1, para. 193)

In alcohol addiction, this is called a "geographical change". This is usually a vain attempt by the alcoholic to explain their alcoholism by blaming it on people, places, and things, and attempting to start afresh with new people in a new environment. It is a futile exercise. There is an A.A. adage, "Wherever you go, there you are". This means that while the environment changes the person remains the same. Not surprisingly for this young man the change of scenery proved of short benefit.

Jung reported that things did not work out in the new firm because the man

> flouted the authority of his uncle who was his chief, annoyed him in every conceivable way, covered him with insults and led an utterly dissolute life, indulging in every kind of excess. He didn't do a stroke of work, and after a few months had to be sent home again as a severe alcoholic. (CW 1, para. 193)

The man "was then put in a home for alcoholics, but paid little attention to the regime of abstinence and used his days out for alcoholic and sexual excess" (Ibid.).

The contempt for authority or more clinically "oppositional defiance" amongst active alcoholics appears to be a common attribute. Defiance is a characteristic of many active alcoholics. This may be related to an inflated ego and sense of narcissistic entitlement fuelled by alcohol.

If an alcoholic does not agree to voluntarily stop drinking, there is little chance of success. Prochaska, Norcross, and DiClemente have written about their concept of "the wheel of change" for a person in addiction and it means simply that a person has to be ready to change (Prochaska, Norcross, & DiClemente, 1994). The wheel of change includes a pre-contemplative and contemplative stage. This in effect means that the pre-contemplative is not even considering giving up drinking. The alcoholic has to be at least in the contemplative stage to succeed in stopping drinking.

Jung wrote about this young man, "In regard to his dipsomania he showed insight, but in regard to its cure he displayed a very shallow optimism. He was convinced of the necessity for abstinence, but overestimated his energy and powers of resistance" (CW 1, para. 194). This is an apt description of the alcoholic who swears off alcohol the "morning after the night before", only to resume the same old pattern of drinking again that evening. Alcoholics who engage in this can convince others simply because they really believe themselves that they will stop drinking "tomorrow". Not surprisingly spouses and partners of alcoholics distance themselves from this insanity. Often a person with an alcohol problem can have a great cognitive understanding of the illogicality of their compulsion to drink; however, neurobiology shows that the impulse to drink may stem from the primitive or reptile brain. If deprived of alcohol, the reptile brain sends distraught signals to the body via tremors and agitation as if warning the body that it is going to die unless it is once again revived with alcohol, hence the strength, unreasonableness, and unmanageability of the craving.

Continuing his case history of this young man, Jung wrote that,

> While in the hospital, he took drawing lessons and apparently riding lessons but gave them up after a few lessons. He realised his superficiality was abnormal and cheerfully admitted it, even priding himself on this specialty of his: "You see, I'm the most cultured and well-read superficial person", he said to me once .... He revelled

in stories of his drinking bouts and other excesses, although there
was nothing in the least praiseworthy about them. (CW 1, para. 194)

In clinical terminology, if the primary illness of alcoholism is not diagnosed then the symptoms of alcoholism can easily be confused with a
range of other emotional problems. In this case there is an inflated ego
with bi-polarity combined with traits of grandiosity, narcissism, oppositional defiance, and *puer aeternus* immaturity. He is using defence
mechanisms that helps distance the ego from the true Self, for example using humour as a defence mechanism to avoid getting in touch
with his true feelings that include pain. In Jungian terms there are also
elements of a wild Dionysian lust for life combined with contempt for
convention.

Jung further wrote,

> Of his former life he lacked all feeling of shame; could talk with
> broad complacency about how he had worried his uncle almost
> sick, and felt no trace of gratitude for him for having taken a great
> deal of trouble to put him on the right road again. (CW 1, para. 194)

Shame is normally a part of the alcoholic's life story. Normally alcoholics will be able to "laugh off" the embarrassments they have caused
rather than acknowledge the hurt they have caused to their families.
Ebby Thacher, Bill Wilson's sponsor, regaled in the following story
about a car crash he was involved in:

> After driving drunkenly into a house, demolishing the gable wall
> and only stopping in the kitchen, he reputedly got out of the car
> and looking at the traumatised woman of the house cowering in the
> corner, asked her, "Any chance of a cup of coffee?" (The Winner's
> Circle, July 2012)

It is such tales of embellished bravado that sustain some drinkers and
support their grandiose delusions of Dionysian revelry. However, the
reality of Ebby's car crash was that it resulted in him appearing before
a judge for committal to an insane asylum. On a serious note, not all
bon homie story tellers survive their car crashes or drinking bouts: The
Welsh poet, Dylan Thomas aged thirty-nine, boasted in the White Horse
Tavern in Greenwich Village "I've had eighteen straight whiskies.
I think this is a record" (Gately, 2008, p. 415). He later went into a coma
from which he never recovered.

*Understanding alcoholism through the case histories of
C. G. Jung: a female alcoholic*

Jung gave detailed background information about another patient, a woman who was first admitted to hospital for alcoholism in 1896. She was in her late thirties when first admitted to the hospital. This appears to be around the average age when female alcoholics begin to hit "rock bottom", for men it is usually around the age of forty. Women alcoholics have a double jeopardy in that they are physically more vulnerable to the effects of alcohol and society is less tolerant than toward men (Bauer, 1982, p. 19).

The case history as outlined below by Jung is a familiar story of self-destruction especially amongst women who have been traumatically abused during childhood and or their adolescence.

Her father was a lawyer and an alcoholic who died of cirrhosis of the liver. According to Jung, her mother died of "some mental illness, apparently paralysis of the insane" (CW 1, para. 197).

Alcoholism can be genetically inherited especially from the paternal line and in this case her mother's illness may have compounded her daughter's alcohol problem, giving her a co-morbid condition or dual diagnosis. However, underlying this diagnosis there was trauma. Jung wrote that, "The first psychopathic symptoms in this hereditarily tainted patient showed themselves from her eighteenth year in the form of marked hysteria resulting from sexual traumata" (CW 1, para. 204). The trauma was caused by an employee of her father's who made two violent attempts to rape her when she was eighteen. Her father was having an extramarital affair, and the perpetrator blackmailed her into not reporting the assaults, threatening that he would "make devastating revelations concerning her father's affairs". She suffered for years from the memory of these assaults and from the continual sexual molestation by this man. She gradually "developed hysterical attacks of convulsion, unaccountable moods, mostly depressions with fits of despair, and to deaden them she began drinking wine. According to her relatives, she was good-natured and soft hearted, but extremely weak-willed". She had married at the age of twenty-two but "the marriage was not a happy one". She felt she was misunderstood by her husband and could never get accustomed to social etiquette. At parties given in their house she secretly slipped away and danced in the yard with the servants. Her husband "started an intimate relationship with the housekeeper. This was enough to aggravate her already excited condition so gravely that she had to be sent to an institution" (CW 1, para. 197).

In this case Jung looks for psychoanalytical precipitating and aggravating causes. In doing so there is the presumption that if these complex traumas are assimilated then the condition of alcoholism would recede. However, the fact is that once alcoholism has taken hold, a rubicon has been crossed and no measure of analytical insight will alleviate the condition. In the same way that a broken leg may have been caused by a fall in the dark, providing light in the future will not heal the existing broken leg.

Jung provides more background information on this young woman. In 1896, while on a day outing, she unexpectedly became engaged to another patient who was also being treated for alcoholism (CW 1, para. 199). According to Jung she lived "in sin" with her fiancée. However her fiancée had a relapse and also "started her off drinking again" (Ibid.).

Usually, alcoholics have the good sense to marry non-alcoholics since they need someone to look after them. Male alcoholics are notorious for choosing caring co-dependent wives, nurses being a favourite "target". When both partners in a marriage are alcoholic then the prognosis is not good since they may end up projecting their own intolerable alcoholic behaviour and emotions onto each other.

Jung continues, later she

> tried to make a living in the grocery trade, but without much success. Once more she took to heavy drinking, got drunk daily, frequented taverns of ill repute, and on one occasion tore off her clothes in a frenzy of excitement, so that she stood there in her petticoat. She often turned up at the tavern dressed only in petticoat and raincoat. (Ibid.)

She returned to the asylum

> On admission she had a hysterical attack with symptoms of *delirium tremens* …. Later she became touchy, flaunted her superior social position before others, was at times erotic, and tried to flirt with a male patient, singing him sentimental songs from a distance. (Ibid.)

While in the hospital she learned typewriting and helped in the anatomical laboratory where she managed to get drunk with laboratory alcohol that was ninety-six per cent proof.

She was discharged on 11 October 1900, and took up a post as a housekeeper. She "worked extraordinarily well and was much appreciated for her continual gaiety and sociability" (Ibid.). At the beginning of July 1901 she became ill with influenza, and "her employer, inadvisably gave her wine as a tonic (!), whereupon she got a bottle of wine sent up every day for a week and on 7 July 1901 she was readmitted to Burghölzli suffering from delirium tremens, having lately drunk methylated spirits and eau de cologne" (CW 1, para. 203).

Jung continues to outline her relevant behaviour.

> At a music rehearsal in the room of an assistant doctor she was "extremely vivacious and talkative, erotic and provocative". She was sexually very excited at this period, but sometimes depressed .... Very sensitive, reacting to censure with deep depression, all emotional reactions extremely labile and immoderate. She had no insight into her lability, greatly overestimated herself and her powers of resistance, had an inflated sense of her personal value, and often made disdainful remarks about other people. She felt she had "a task in front of her" and "was destined for something higher and better". (CW 1, para. 203)

It is as though this young woman's ego is saying that settling for an ordinary position of being "a worker amongst workers" is not acceptable and rebels by disturbing the peace. In previous times, her "hysterical" behaviour might have resulted in her being burnt as a witch! This patient was arguably what is now termed "the identified patient", and sending her to an asylum or an Irish-type Magdalene laundry was and is an expedient solution for a "respectable family." Possibly the reason for society's comparative intolerance of women alcoholics is because of the male shadow side that depends upon women to be sober and moral in their relationships as well as reliable in their child bearing and rearing.

CHAPTER FOUR

How A.A. works

A.A. preamble

Alcoholics Anonymous is a fellowship of men and women who share their experience, strength, and hope with each other that they may solve their common problem and help others to recover from alcoholism. The only requirement for membership is a desire to stop drinking. There are no dues or fees for A.A. membership; we are self-supporting through our own contributions. A.A. is not allied with any sect, denomination, politics, organization or institution; does not wish to engage in any controversy; neither endorses nor opposes any causes. Our primary purpose is to stay sober and help other alcoholics to achieve sobriety. (The "A.A. Preamble," copyright 1958 by the A.A. Grapevine, Inc. Reprinted by kind permission.)

The above preamble is a succinct introduction to Alcoholics Anonymous. Its purpose is to describe briefly the principles, procedures, and functions of A.A. It is read at the beginning of most A.A. meetings. It was written by the editor of the A.A. *Grapevine* magazine in 1947 and was based on the foreword to the original edition of the Big Book, *Alcoholics Anonymous*.

The first sentence of the preamble encapsulates the essence of the A.A. programme, in particular that it is a fellowship. A fellowship is defined as a "society of people sharing mutual interest or activities" (*Collins English Dictionary*, 2011). A secondary definition includes "companionship or friendship". These features are definitely a part of Alcoholics Anonymous. The first sentence relates to sharing of experiences, strengths and hopes with other fellow alcoholics. Sharing of experience is the cornerstone of A.A. and goes back to that day in the Mayflower Hotel, Akron Ohio, in May 1935, when Bill Wilson decided to seek out another alcoholic so as to share his experiences of alcoholism. Wilson found that sharing his experience with another alcoholic connected him to a support that enabled him to resist the compulsion to drink. The sharing of strength and hope reminds the alcoholic of the immense benefits of giving up alcohol. This sharing with a fellow sufferer has a remarkable effect. It's as though the spirit of the Biblical quote comes into force: "For where two or three have gathered together in My name, I am there in their midst" (Matthew, 18:20, Gideon Edition).

When first contemplating joining A.A., many people think that they have to stand up in a large group and say that they are an alcoholic. In fact all that is required for membership is, as stated in the second sentence of the preamble, "is a desire to stop drinking". This is significant in that a person does not need to self-diagnose themselves as being an alcoholic. This is to encourage newcomers so they do not have to get into the debating society of what constitutes being an alcoholic. Indeed there is no agreed medical definition of alcoholism. Some members even after twenty years may occasionally ruminate as to whether they are really an alcoholic or not. Some even test the waters again. However, while there are some professional descriptions of the illness of alcoholism, it is left to the person with an alcohol problem to decide themselves whether they are an alcoholic.

In practice it is possible at a meeting, if asked by anybody to introduce yourself or to speak, to simply say, "Pass". Ideally a newcomer will not be asked directly. However, after a while most people will introduce themselves and say, "My name is … and I am an alcoholic". However this really is for convenience and technically it should be possible to simply say "my name is … and I have a desire to stop drinking". Members making this opening statement are reinforcing and acknowledging that they are alcoholic.

Some people joining A.A. may consider that there is a trick, for example, that A.A. is a religious cult or is out to get money from people desperate for an answer to their problem. So, the third sentence states explicitly that there are no membership fees; indeed there is a cap on the maximum annual financial contribution a member may make, which is approximately $3,000. Alcoholics Anonymous is self-funding, so there are no membership forms to fill in for subsidies or funding and this helps A.A. retain the principle of anonymity. The mention that it is fully self-supporting is a hint that a small contribution towards rent and heating is normally expected. This is a good idea because it immediately gives the newcomer a sense of being part of the group, that their membership is important, and they are a part of a mutual self-help organisation that needs them as well as them needing it. The astonishing thing about A.A. and what differentiates it from other organisations is that it deliberately tries to remain non-professional except for some paid professional staff. The organisation relies on its members to act not as bosses, but instead to act as servants to the group. Overall, while many new members at their first meeting report a sense of anxiety, they also report that they felt they had come home. Indeed they no longer feel apart from, but instead feel a part of something.

The A.A. preamble states categorically that it has no alliance with any "sect, denomination, politics, organization or institution", nor wishes to become involved in any ideologies. Effectively this means that all are welcome regardless of colour, class, sex, or creed. While most organisations have an agenda or act as pressure groups, the reason A.A. deliberately refrains from becoming involved in outside issues is so that it can focus on the "primary purpose" of staying sober and helping other alcoholics to achieve sobriety, especially the newcomer. The following section outlines how A.A. meetings are organised and what usually happens inside an A.A. meeting.

How A.A. meetings are organised

Firstly ordinary members locate a room, usually in a community hall or more usually in a church. Symbolically, most of these rooms appear to be in basements! A rent is agreed and is usually paid weekly or monthly. Because A.A. is self-financing, "free" rent may be a contradiction of Tradition seven, which states that "every group ought to be self-supporting" (see Appendix Five). If a meeting cannot afford the weekly rent or does not have members who are prepared to give their service freely as secretaries or treasurers, then it simply closes.

Once the room is found a small closet is usually made available where A.A. literature and large scrolls of the twelve steps and twelve traditions can be stored. Since each group is self-supporting, the scrolls and literature are purchased by the group.

The meeting is organised in the following way. They usually take place weekly in the same room and normally last an hour in cities and in some rural areas an hour and a half. A secretary is elected by the group from amongst its members and they normally rotate every three to twelve months. The secretary normally is responsible for inviting a speaker, called "the chair", to speak. The "chair" is a recovering alcoholic and they speak for ten to thirty minutes on their experience, strength and hope. The secretary opens the meeting by welcoming members, and anyone back from a "slip", and asks if any new member would like to introduce themselves so the group can get to know them, as opposed to embarrassing them. The Big Book understands that, "We are people who normally would not mix. But there exists among us a fellowship, friendliness, and an understanding which is indescribably wonderful" (Anon, 1991a, p. 17). So going along for the first time may be worrying, in that people may have experienced going into a group of strangers for the first time, maybe a party or a parent-teacher meeting, where everyone automatically pairs up and they are left alone, but that is rarely the case at an A.A. meeting: There is a sensitivity whereby newcomers are generally acknowledged and welcomed. Indeed most people remember the welcome on their first visit and the feeling of being at home!

It would appear that grandiosity is a trait associated with alcoholics (Anon, 2002, p. 127). So it is not surprising that it appears that a disproportionally high number of people with alcohol problems are agnostics or atheists. For them, the fact that the word "God" is mentioned three times in the twelve steps may offend them. They may decide to give up immediately. For some, who have been abused by their fathers, the Lord's Prayer at the end of some meetings may put salt in their wounds.

One twelve-step member who attended a meeting relating to eating problems wrote about his experience of his first meeting:

My rational mind was dead set against returning, principally because of the God stuff. But some other part of me wanted to see and hear more. The more emotional side of me had been moved by what I had experienced; I had felt a sense of validation and common experience. I knew that, for an hour and a half, I had spent time with a community of people who knew the hell I had been going through for years. I wanted more contact with that community. So, despite my discomfort with the God talk and the prayers, I resolved to go to meetings and take their suggestions, at least for a while. (Z, 1990, pp. 21–22)

The next stage of the opening of the meeting is when the secretary asks a member to read the preamble, which is a succinct introduction to how the fellowship works. Following the reading of the preamble another member may read, "How it Works"—this explains how A.A. works and includes the twelve steps of A.A. (see Appendix Four). The secretary will then ask if anyone would like to raise any issue relating to A.A. business—a member may inform the group of a new meeting or alteration of the time of a meeting or about a local or national convention of A.A.

The "chair" may then be introduced. The "chair" is the first speaker and for ten to thirty minutes they share their experience, strength, and hope and "what we were like, what happened, and what we are like now". The meeting is then opened for other members present who may wish to share what is happening for them. The member wishing to speak introduces themselves by their first name: "My name is Mary and I am an alcoholic", and other members in unison say, "Hi Mary" and at the end of the share, "Thank you Mary". This gives a feeling of being heard, acknowledged and accepted.

While there are no rules in A.A., there are conventions, the main one being that no member comments adversely on what another person says, called "a share". This is known as cross-sharing. Sometimes a misunderstanding of this convention prevents members from offering supportive words to another person's share or at a minimum when offering support beginning with, "I don't mean to cross-share but ..."

Toward the end of the meeting, the secretary brings the meeting to a close, usually by saying "unless anyone has a burning desire to share I will bring the meeting to an end" and then asks a member to read the promises (see Appendix Four). Then a cup, box, basket, or hat is passed around for a collection. The secretary will normally refer to the seventh tradition that states, "We are self-supporting, declining outside contributions." The collection is used to pay the rent and help with providing literature for prisons and the balance may be sent to intergroup for eventual forwarding to headquarters. The rent for A.A. headquarters in New York is approximately $60,000 a month and the salaries for the eighty-five staff approaches six million dollars a year.

Meetings in America and Ireland usually end with the Lord's Prayer and the Serenity Prayer "for those who wish to say them". In Britain, the Lord's Prayer is not used as much in deference to multiculturalism. All meetings end with the short version of the group Serenity Prayer and it is usually introduced as, "We will end with the Serenity Prayer using God as you understand Him". The words of the group Serenity Prayer are: "God, grant us the serenity to accept the things we cannot change, the courage to change the things we can, and wisdom to know the difference" (Anon, 2002, p. 130).

The plural "us" and "we" is used to symbolise that the meeting is united and supportive. The twelfth step suggest that members use the plural term in acknowledgment that they are part of a whole, yet most members, out of habit, still use the singular pronoun "I" rather than "we" or "us" (Anon, 2002, p. 130). Following the Serenity Prayer members usually say, "Keep coming back, it works if you work it, so work it, you're worth it!".

When the meeting is over, tea or coffee is normally served. This custom came from Akron, Ohio, when members used to go to a doughnut shop after the meetings. However, some members could not afford the cost, so it was decided that tea and coffee should be offered after each meeting.

Ironically, Bill Wilson, in his final writings, wrote of his concern of the addiction to caffeine and biscuits during meetings and nicotine which some members use after the meetings.

The following chapter will give a synopsis of the twelve steps of A.A.

CHAPTER FIVE

A synopsis of the twelve steps

A synopsis of the twelve steps

This synopsis of the twelve steps shows how they are a gentle introduction primarily towards healing the Self. There are four main themes to the steps; admission of powerlessness over alcohol, confession of misdeeds and character defects associated with alcoholism, making amends to family, colleagues, and friends, and having completed the exercises, then putting them into action by being of service to others, in particular to still-suffering alcoholics.

Step one. We admitted we were powerless over alcohol—that our lives had become unmanageable

The first part of step one asks the person to acknowledge their powerlessness over alcohol, that it has power over them and that they have lost their power to control alcohol. Once the first drink is taken there is a compulsion to continue drinking. There is a popular adage that encapsulates this process: "First the man takes the drink, then the drink takes a drink, then the drink takes the man".

The second part of this step reinforces the first part and highlights the reality that alcohol is at the centre of the life of the alcoholic and it is managing them and making their lives unmanageable. Alcohol may be their *raison d'etre* for working; as Oscar Wilde said, "Work is the curse of the drinking classes" (www.goodreads.com). Managing life for the primary purpose of drinking does not qualify as managing life.

Step two. Came to believe that a Power greater than ourselves could restore us to sanity

Many alcoholics disagree with the usual childlike concept of a God in the Heavens, but most will agree there may be a mysterious power out there in the Universe that is greater than themselves. After some months of sobriety, there dawns a realisation that even a token belief in some power greater than themselves is helping to keep them sober and sane. I have heard members say that although they were atheists at the time, they got down on their knees, raised their hands to the Heavens and beseeched an unknown presence to relieve them of their addiction to alcohol and it worked! They felt that relenting even partially on their intellectual agnostic or atheistic beliefs was a small price to pay for their sobriety.

The second part of this step refers to sanity. Most alcoholics would rightly be reluctant to describe themselves as insane. While the term "sanity" is used colloquially, many alcoholics might agree that they are not quite normal, indeed might even agree that their lifestyle is a bit on the wild side. Still more would agree with the definition that continuing to do the same thing repeatedly (drinking) and hoping to get a different result (not getting drunk) is a practical definition of insanity. Finally, after some time of sobriety most alcoholics looking back at their drinking bouts might agree that their drinking was indeed "mad".

Step three. Made a decision to turn our will and our lives over to the care of God as we understood Him

As with most of the steps they are interlinked; step three is directly related to step two and is a progression from coming to believe in a 'Power greater that ourselves' to a turning of 'our will and our lives over to the care of God'. However, turning lives over to the care of God is not the complete surrender it implies, more so an admission that there is a Higher Power that cares and can help. That Higher Power can be the supportive power of the A.A. group who have been able to do what the individual cannot do alone.

The words *as we understood Him* were included in the third step so as to emphasise that A.A. does not have a definition of God. Despite referring to "Him" it is up to each individual member of A.A. to try and find their own concept of God and it can of course be a "Her" or an "It" or a universal spiritual energy.

Step four. Made a searching and fearless moral inventory of ourselves

The first three steps are about admitting powerlessness over alcohol and deciding that there is a God-like Higher Power or energy that is greater than the ego of the alcoholic. Part of working the programme of the twelve steps is about trying to become a better human being, not becoming perfect. In order to make progress it is necessary to become conscious of any fears, resentments, and character flaws so as to remedy, purge, or even tolerate them. The usual way to become conscious of these fears and defects is to write them down. They can be put under the normal human failings of the seven deadly sins of pride, greed, lust, anger, gluttony, envy, and sloth. This list may illuminate underlying common factors, such as threats to financial security and self-esteem that may trigger drinking.

It should be borne in mind that while the inventory will highlight the dark shadow areas of the personality, it is likely that positive aspects will also emerge, not least a willingness to learn and to change for the better.

Step five. Admitted to God, to ourselves, and to another human being the exact nature of our wrongs

Once character defects are written down, it is then suggested that this is followed by telling them to a trusted confidante, ideally someone who is experienced in hearing fifth steps and most importantly can cope with the information and not disclose it to another as gossip. Many people choose their sponsors, and others look outside the fellowship to a trusted friend or priest. People report that once they have found the right person and revealed everything there was to know about them, then the reward was an immense feeling of freedom. People often say that when making their fifth step, they told a secret that they fully intended on taking to the grave. There is a general axiom that your secrets will keep you sick, and in AA it is said that your secrets will make you drink again. When sharing their personal stories with a sponsor, many people remark that whatever their guilty secret was, their sponsor was able to "top it" with one of their own stories, and it was that identification that made them feel their character defects were a part of being human. Prior to a fifth step, shame may have separated the alcoholic from the community of humanity and the elimination of this shame facilitates a reunion with themselves, families, and community.

Step Six. Were entirely ready to have God remove all these defects of character

Steps four and five will help a person to discover their shortcomings which includes alcoholism combined with the seven deadly sins. During steps four and five, defects of character will have been written down and then confessed to another human being. While sharing secrets in step five will alleviate feelings of guilt and give a sense of freedom, defects of character will still remain. There is a saying in A.A. that an alcoholic horse thief who gives up drinking is still a horse thief. Indeed defects of character may be enjoyable, for example, becoming angry may give some people a temporary high. Step six is simply a gentle and subtle preparation to become "entirely ready" to have these defects of character removed. It is about gaining a willingness to change. Becoming "entirely ready" is emphasised, as half-measures will not work. The next step involves asking God as we "understood Him" to actually remove these shortcomings.

Step seven. Humbly asked Him to remove our shortcomings

The newcomer may feel that there is a stigma to attending A.A. Crossing the threshold of an A.A. meeting is a daunting prospect and may be experienced as a humiliation. In reality the degree of humiliation will not match that experienced while drinking. However, once across the A.A. parapet, people report that they felt welcomed. Members of all ranks, captains of industry, movie stars and even the less fortunate generally accept each other as ordinary co-equal members of the human race. It's as though in A.A. there is a realisation that no matter what a person's status, everybody is a spiritual being in a material body. Ironically, after a while, the new members may feel sorry for non-alcoholics who don't have such an enriching programme to guide them in their life.

New members will see that shortcomings have been removed from other members. They might remember and realise that getting down on their knees and asking "Him" for help was a humble gesture that was successful in relieving them of their craving for alcohol. So again they may humble themselves and ask their Higher Power to remove their shortcomings. Again they may feel this humble gesture is a small price to pay. Overall becoming humble will include getting rid of alcohol-fuelled grandiosity, arrogance, and a delusional sense of one's self-importance in the world.

Step eight. Made a list of all persons we had harmed, and became willing to make amends to them all

This list is similar to the one already composed in step four, where a "searching and fearless moral inventory of ourselves" was made. Now at step eight other people are included in the list. These normally are family members, neighbours, and work colleagues who had been upset, hurt or harmed. The first part of step eight involves writing out a list of people harmed. There may be a reluctance to admit that others were harmed, but generally a realisation comes that drinking did affect others adversely.

The second part of step eight clearly states, "and became willing to make amends". This step is a gentle introduction in that it only asks for a willingness to make amends to people who have been harmed. It is a preparatory step towards action that is required in step nine.

Step nine. Made direct amends to such people whenever possible, except when to do so would injure them or others

Step nine, involves putting steps four, five, and eight into action. It involves approaching people who have been hurt or harmed and making appropriate amends. It is important to note that making amends involves not just apologising but also involves, wherever possible, restitution. It is advised that caution be exercised because rushing to make amends can make matters worse. This is a step that has to be undertaken with sensitivity and thoughtfulness and is best done in consultation with a sponsor or trusted advisor.

Most people making amends comment on the goodwill they receive from their "victims"; debts are waived and harms done are willingly forgiven and forgotten. Generally most recipients of these amends wish the recovering alcoholic well and are grateful for the sincerity. Overall, step nine is about the recovering alcoholic cleaning their side of the street.

Step ten. Continued to take personal inventory and when we were wrong promptly admitted it

This step is a reminder to keep a daily watch on personal interactions with others so as to ensure that others are treated fairly. Recovering alcoholics are advised that admitting wrongfulness to another is a chance to exercise humility; a prompt admission of wrongdoing prevents the building up of false defences to justify unfair actions. Ironically, an admission of being in the wrong can deflate the "opposition" as they may be stunned by such an unusual stance. Avoiding arguments and fights is proof that as stated in the Big Book, "We have ceased fighting anything or anyone—even alcohol", and have "entered the world of the Spirit" (Anon, 1991a, p. 84). Following step ten, the next two steps are about putting the knowledge learned in the previous ten steps into practice.

Step eleven. Sought through prayer and meditation to increase our conscious contact with God as we understand Him, praying only for knowledge of His will for us and the power to carry that out

In order to maintain what has been learned, this step encourages the practice of prayer and meditation. Prayer involves talking with the Higher Power and asking for support and guidance to get through the day. Meditation involves listening to the inner Self and gaining an intuitive understanding of what God's will is. It is advised humourously by members of A.A. that shoes are stored underneath the bed as this will entail kneeling down at night and again kneeling in the morning when retrieving the shoes. While there "we ask God to direct our thinking" for the remainder of the day (Ibid., p. 86).

Step twelve. Having had a spiritual awaking as a result of these steps, we tried to carry this message to alcoholics, and to practice these principles in all our affairs

The Big Book devotes more pages to explaining step twelve than to any other step. This signifies its importance. Notably, this step states that as a result of working the previous eleven steps a spiritual awakening occurs. This awakening is a gradual process and is elusive and cannot be easily defined. Friends and family members may recognise that a change for the better has occurred in the recovering alcoholic, particularly that they are less selfish and of course are not drinking. They themselves may feel happier, serene, and more comfortable in their own skin.

The chapter in the Big Book that covers this step is entitled, "Working with others", and is about putting the spiritual knowledge into action. The success of A.A. is built upon the premise of one alcoholic talking with another, one wounded healer helping another. It is a co-equal relationship and is different than being "counselled" by doctors and therapists who may not have firsthand experience of the illness of alcoholism. Accordingly, the Big Book encourages recovering alcoholics in A.A. to reach out to the still suffering alcoholic: "You can help when no one else can" (Ibid., p. 89).

The following chapter elaborates on the twelve steps using narratives from recovering alcoholics combined with a Jungian and A.A. perspective.

Step one

We admitted we were powerless over alcohol—that our lives had become unmanageable

The graphic narratives below are from recovering alcoholics who are members of A.A. and have written their stories for the monthly A.A. magazine *Share*. The names of the contributors have been changed to protect their identities. Their stories give a true flavour of the long battle with alcohol that finally leads to admitting powerlessness over alcohol commonly referred to as hitting "rock bottom". Rock bottom usually means the turning point when the person has nowhere else to go and then appeals to any energy in the universe that might help. While it appears there is a choice for the alcoholic, the reality is that it may be a

choice between life and death. Niall's story is typical of an alcoholic's
first reaction to an A.A. meeting:

> I first dabbled with A.A. in 2005 where I attended six meetings and
> decided that A.A. wasn't for me. In my second meeting I looked
> down at the scrolls and when I saw the word "God" in step three
> I thought I was sitting in some sort of cult. I didn't bother to look
> at step twelve; I immediately assumed it was a suicide pact! When
> the pot was passed around it reminded me of church and I thought
> that their real aim was to get my money! I was 32 at the time and
> my head kept telling me, "I've got more drinking left in me and I'm
> not that bad". I heard a man share that he hadn't had a drink for ten
> years and that frightened me more than the "God" word. So after
> my sixth meeting in 2005 I decided A.A. wasn't for me and that I
> could stop on my own. (*Share*, May 2014, p. 27)

Ben, a recovering alcoholic describes his last "rock bottom" days:

> Beset by fear and paranoia I was ill and not working. There
> had been disputes with family members, work colleagues, my
> employer, trades people, and solicitors. Disputes with everyone I
> was in contact with. (*Share*, January 2012, pp. 6–7)

Fred's story:

> Being gay I spent a lot of time in bars and clubs … I regularly got
> ripped off finding my wallet empty in the morning but still went
> out for more. I was dying and knew it, yet I still carried on; until
> one night I cried for help and it came in the form of a very physical
> spiritual experience. I awoke 24 hours later in hospital where I was
> told I had been found collapsed in the street, I have no memory of
> this but the compulsion to drink had gone somehow. I believe now
> it was a miracle. (*Share*, March 2013, pp. 24–26)

Jack wrote of the choices he was left with:

> I could kill myself, drink again or try A.A. Luckily for me, I tried
> my last idea first, called the local helpline and went to a meeting—
> what a fantastic feeling that was. I knew that evening from the
> shares (what people talk about) and the welcome, to know that for
> me, I had come home. (*Share*, January 2012, p. 3)

Bert said he:

Always believed that you measured your success by how far you climbed up the ladder and how you see that was by the amount of money you had, the house you had and the car you drove. Those were the things I believed in. I went to A.A. but couldn't get the message. What changed my mind was this. Pope Paul was visiting Dublin. I'd promised my ten-year-old son I would bring him along to the Phoenix Park. I arrived home drunk at lunch and my son was dressed up in his scout's uniform. I asked him "where are you going kiddo?" My wife came out of the kitchen and said "you bastard, you're supposed to bring us up to see the Pope today." My son was asthmatic and we had talked about that, by bringing him up to see the Pope he might get the cure for the asthma. I had failed again and let him down again. My wife looked at me in disgust and out they went. I turned on the TV and looked at the man, he was down in Galway speaking to the young people of Ireland and he said it's a hot day after this I am going in to have a cool lager. And I said to myself even the Pope can have a drink and I can't. And I haven't had a drink since that day and that was on the on 27th September 1979, something happened to me on that day, whatever it was I saw the failure. I really was letting my family down on that day. Two or three days later I went up to see my doctor in St. Dymphna's hospital and told him I want to really stop this time and I mean it—he looked at me and said, "you're serious" and I said I am and I told him what happened to my son. He said OK I'm going to put you on antabuse tablets and you come up here every day he said and I said I can't afford to do that, it costs me two buses to get here and he said I'm going to give you a bus pass and he arranged for a bus pass for me, the whole lot. I went up to that man every day, now he says I want you to go home and sit down and play with your son and I arrived back home and I look at her and him the young fella and sat down and started to play with him—one of the hardest things I had to do I found was sit down and play with my son. After one minute I was bored stiff and I got up and said to her I can't do this for him you know. I went up to the doctor and I told him "I can't do it" and he said "you better learn how to do it, you've been given one chance, take it don't let it go" and I went back home again and started playing with him, very hard thing to do, then I started bringing him to school and then I started doing things for him, this, that and the other and after about two year [sic] of bringing him to school, he said to me one morning when I said to him come on kiddo, let's go, we're nearly late "I'm going with the boys today Da," so I said "What do you mean you're going with the boys that's my job", "no" he says "I'm going with the boys" and you know something I was shocked I was losing me job, shocked me you know, she turned to me and says "you have to let him go". My son is 46 now and he is my closest buddy. (Personal interview, 20 February 2014)

John:

I was always trying to give it up, swore off the drink everytime I woke up with a hangover, room spinning and feeling sick, but by the following evening always thought that maybe this time I could control it and just have a few drinks. Then I tried every permutation to control my drinking, drank only after 6pm or if at lunch diluted white wine and then tried drinking only sherry after 9 p.m. Even tried to limit myself to only four pints a night but would exceed that and drink tomorrow's four pints as well and then try to limit myself to only 20 pints a week and then I would exceed that limit and borrow next weeks' quota and bring it forward to the week I was drinking in. Often decided that tonight would be different and I would drive my car to the pub and only have two pints. After the fifth pint I'd worry about driving home so would plan to bring clean urine with me next time so that if stopped by the police while driving I could pour the tube of urine into their bottle. The next morning I would wake with the usual hangover and think that was an immoral plan, the answer was simple, I would simply stop drinking. But by the next evening I would decide again in the same cycle of self-delusion that I could limit my drinking to two pints. I was forever stopping and starting drinking so the merry go round continued and I felt I was in the middle of it without any control over my drinking. (Personal interview, 15 August 2013)

Explanation

Effectively step one asks for a full admission "to our innermost selves that we were (are) [author's insert] alcoholics" (Anon, 1991a, p. 30).

The first word of step one is inclusive, the step, as it is written, begins with the word "We". It is clear about the need to admit powerlessness over alcohol; it is this admission of powerlessness over alcohol which is needed if there is to be the possibility of recovery. Denial is a part of the illness and addiction is supposedly the only illness that tells a person they don't have it. Bill Wilson wrote in the A.A. book, *Twelve Steps and Twelve Traditions*, "The principle that we shall find no enduring strength until we first admit complete defeat is the main taproot from which our whole society has sprung and flowered" (Anon, 2002, p. 22).

An excerpt from the *Twelve Steps and Twelve Traditions*, asks,

> Why all this insistence that every A.A. must hit bottom first? The answer is that few people will sincerely try to practice the A.A. program unless they have hit bottom .... Under the lash of alcoholism, we are driven to A.A. and there we discover the fatal nature of our situation. Then, and only then, do we become open-minded to conviction and as willing to listen as the dying can be. We stand ready to do anything that will lift the merciless obsession from us. (Anon, 2002, p. 24)

Powerlessness over alcohol occurs in the life of every alcoholic. It is the tipping point; once the rubicon of addictive drinking is crossed there can be no return to normal social drinking. There is an extreme element of illogicality in the person with an alcohol problem when it comes to reasoning about their drinking. They may believe that next time they drink it will be different. Then as they reach for the glass they fool themselves with the thought that they will stop after a few drinks. However, with a drink on board, they are a different person from the one who started drinking, so when the few drinks are finished, they will say to themselves, "In for a penny in for a pound". Thoughts of a partner who will be annoyed may be supplanted by "might as well get hung for a sheep as a lamb".

Bill Wilson underlined his explanation of the alcoholics' powerlessness over alcohol:

> Our so-called will power becomes practically non-existent. We are unable at certain times, to bring into our consciousness with sufficient force the memory of the suffering and humiliation of even a week or month ago. We are without defence against the first drink. (Anon, 2011, p. 43)

The first step is usually divided into two parts and there is a hyphen linking the two parts of the sentence. The second part of the first step suggests that there be an admission that "our lives had become unmanageable". Some people may not see this unmanageability because their partners may be managing their lives for them. This unmanageability is linked to a feeling of wanting to throw in the towel. In A.A. it is called reaching "rock bottom", and it is a decisive point, sometimes called feeling sick and tired of being sick and tired. Entering A.A. for the first time is a mini-death of the ego but is compensated for by a liberation of the Self, which brings a new freedom and release from the bondage of addictive drinking.

Jungian perspective

William James (1982) wrote about the experience of the ego letting go and trusting in the Higher Power, or the Self: "Believing that a higher power will take care of us in certain ways better than we take care of ourselves, if we only genuinely throw ourselves upon it and consent to use it" (James, 1982, p. 103). James may have been the first to use the term "Higher Power," as a euphemism for God. That expression "Higher Power" is now widely used in A.A.

The first step of Alcoholics Anonymous involves an admission of powerlessness which in Jungian psychology is akin to an admission by the ego that it has been overpowered. It is the first psychological break-through that allows the Self to begin to emerge. The process involved can also be understood as an alchemical metaphor for the individuation process, which can make one whole (Mannion, 1991). The alchemical process allows the true Self, which is imprisoned by the spirit alcohol, to be released.

This first stage in the alchemical process is called the nigredo stage, which means blackness. From an alchemical perspective reaching "rock bottom" or being in the midst of the dark night of the soul, is equivalent to the alchemical process of *nigredo* (Hopeke, 1989, p. 165). In terms of recovery, "rock bottom" is when an alcoholic finally is forced to become aware that their life is not being lived in a healthy manner, either spiritually or physically.

Reaching "rock bottom" may mean that the lesser ego may be deflated enough to give way to the true Self. This can be the beginning of the process whereby the alcoholic stops drinking and begins their first step in fulfilling their true spiritual potential. The next stage in the alchemical process is the albedo.

The *albedo* stage involves the washing away of impurities; this involves a separation process which divides "the pure from the impure" (Abraham, 1998, p. 180). This process necessitates a mini death of the old way of being, "mortification"—this "death of the metal" allows it to be dissolved back into its original form, the *"prima materia"*. This allows the soul (true Self) to be released and the remnants (false ego) sink to the bottom of the containing vessel. According to Abraham, the albedo stage is where the "body has been whitened and spiritualized in preparation to receive illumination from the spirit" in the next and final stage (Ibid., p. 5).

During the last stage, the rubedo (reddening) stage, "the limited lunar consciousness, the brain, receives the full illumination of the spiritual sun" (Ibid., p. 174). This may come in the form of a moment of clarity and may be the beginning of a spiritual awakening.

The alchemical process needs a strong container to hold the burning metal. Similarly, in order to help transform the alcoholic, the A.A. meetings provide a strong "leak proof" vessel that can contain the trickster-ish and mercurial nature of the illness. The structure of the twelve step meetings are supported by the twelve traditions of A.A. (see Appendix Two). In turn the recovery process involves a strong commitment to regularly attend the twelve step meetings, to "work" the steps, offer service and seek the support of a sponsor. Whether it's a sponsor or an analyst, both should be aware that "The alchemist thought that the *opus* demanded not only laboratory work, the reading of books, meditation, and patience, but also love" (CW 16, para. 490).

From a Jungian perspective the admission of powerlessness in step one and the belief in a Higher Power is a form of "death" of the false material ego and "rebirth" of the supremacy of the true spiritual Self over the ego. During this process the ego does not die, it realises it is not God and submits to the greater wisdom of the Self. This descent and assent is a necessary transformative part of the individuation process.

While the first step involves a submission or mini-death of the ego the second step is about renewal, the beginning of rebirth.

Step two

Came to believe that a Power greater than ourselves
could restore us to sanity

Some newcomers complain about the "old fashioned" terminology of A.A. Atheists may dislike the inclusion of the word God; women may dislike the emphasis on the usage of male terminology; African Americans may dislike middle-class white American men telling them they have to admit their powerlessness; and Muslims, Hindus, and Jews may dislike the Christian slant. Gay people may dislike the assumption of heterosexuality. However, it is advised that these issues should temporarily be set aside and that the focus be applied to alcoholism as a life-threatening illness that ruins lives.

One Jewish lady related to me that upon hearing there were no "dues or fees" for A.A. membership, she decided to conceal her religion in order to gain sobriety. Similarly as is illustrated in the following story there is a willingness to go to any lengths to achieve sobriety.

Anne:

> I am a Protestant from Belfast who found myself in an A.A. meeting in Dublin in the church hall in a Catholic chapel. I actually thought I would have to convert to Catholicism in order to get sober. The funny thing was I was willing to do anything to get sober including changing my religion! (*Share*, March 2013, p. 5)

This exemplifies the axiom that "we must be willing to go to any lengths to get sober!" However such lengths are neither expected, suggested or required. The only change that A.A. requires is an internal change, a spiritual change, and not a religious change. Indeed people experiencing a "rock bottom" are usually desperate enough to try anything, including suicide. Many members look back on their drinking days and describe them as insane.

John:

> Well, never thought of myself as insane but in the context of drinking and giving up, suppose doing the same thing over and over again like thinking I could control my drinking and stop after one, two or three and never ever learning that I couldn't is a good definition of insanity—not learning from my many mistakes. That is one of the lessons you learn in A.A., but really to do with my ego—thought I was the centre of the world and the meetings help reduce the size of my ego by being in a room with ordinary people, and realising that I too am ordinary. Once I didn't have to prove anything to these people I felt more at peace once I accepted that. I thought I had to achieve greatness to be accepted but that was

related to satisfying my mother, a teacher, to get her love which was never there and I have to accept that she did the best she could coming from where she came from, just like myself and many others. So I became a part of humanity rather than being apart from it. Certainly, once I stopped drinking my anxieties left me and suppose I always considered myself mad because of the panic attacks and phobias, little did I realise that they were probably brought on by alcohol destroying my nervous system, so today I am generally well balanced throughout the day and to maintain that balance I don't drink or smoke or even take caffeine. I sleep regularly and peacefully at night! (Personal interview, 15 August 2013)

Edward:

> After attending A.A. I had done what the Big Book suggested if I was not convinced I was an alcoholic: Somewhere in the Big Book it says if you are not sure "Step over to the nearest bar-room and try some controlled drinking". That's what I did and that's what convinced me .... I said I would only drink lager with whiskey, which I did and that was how I ended up in a police cell. I came to, rolled off a wooden bed with a wooden pillow on to my knees onto a wet concrete floor, the wet was my urine ... I hope no one else needs to try it and that they are convinced by the first time they come to A.A .... By God's grace I got back to an A.A. meeting that same Sunday I was let out of jail. (*Share*, February 2013, p. 5)

Explanation

Step two is linked to step one in that, "Our lives had become unmanageable", is a polite way of saying that the active alcoholic does insane things, behaves irrationally and can jeopardise his own life, reputation, financial, and emotional wellbeing. Bill Wilson wrote that the second step is "The beginning of the end of his old life, and the beginning of his emergence into a new one" (Anon, 2002, p. 26).

Indeed, while working as a therapist, I've found that some clients have felt that in giving up alcohol, a part of themselves was dying. In one case a client, rather than tell his family that he was coming to see me for advice on his alcohol problem, instead told them he was going to a funeral. There is no doubt that there was some symbolic significance in his choice of subterfuge. Giving up alcohol can seem like a bereavement caused by the loss of the crutch of alcohol, or the possible death of the old way of life.

Step two requires the person with an alcohol problem to accept that change is needed in their life. This can simply begin with an acceptance that there is a Higher Power in the universe. According to Bill Wilson:

> We needed to ask ourselves but one short question.—"Do I now believe, or am I even willing to believe, that there is a Power greater than myself?" As soon as a man can say that he does believe, or is willing to believe, we emphatically assure him that he is on his way. It has been repeatedly proven among us that upon this simple cornerstone, a wonderfully effective spiritual structure can be built. (Anon, 1991a, p. 47)

Overall, step two is about the new member believing in a Higher Power who will help restore them to sanity. The belief in a Higher Power is the foundation for transformation to psychological rebirth.

However, belief in a Higher Power can be objectionable to some new members: "As psychiatrists have often observed, defiance is the outstanding characteristic of many an alcoholic. So it's not strange that lots of us have had our day at defying God Himself" (Anon, 2002, p. 31). Bill Wilson recounts how he was skeptical about religion and "the burnings and chicanery that religious disputes had facilitated, made me sick" (Anon, 2011, p. 37). Step two is a hurdle in that it asks the new member who may be an atheist or agnostic to believe in a Higher Power, albeit of their own understanding. Wilson believes that people entering A.A. may be faced with the fallacy of their defiance, "No man, we saw, could believe in God and defy Him too. Belief meant reliance not defiance. In A.A., we saw the fruits of this belief: men and women spared from alcohol's final catastrophe" (Anon, 2002, p. 32).

Jungian perspective

Carl Jung advised Rowland Hazard that no further medical or psychiatric treatment could help him and only a spiritual transformation could overcome his alcoholism (see Appendix One). Effectively the prescription was that Rowland needed to believe in a spiritual power greater than himself. As Bill Wilson learned his own self-will alone would not work.

Before admitting himself for the fourth time to Towns Hospital for a detox, Bill Wilson left a note on the kitchen table promising his wife: "This time it will be different". Lois' response was that not only did she not believe him, but she was contemptuous and annoyed at the expense entailed for yet another hospitalisation. But, Bill did finally get sober. While in hospital he had a spiritual or in Jungian terms a numinous experience. Such an experience is "psychologically associated with experiences of the Self" (Sharp, 1991, p. 92). This experience may appear to be emanating from an external source. It is described by Jung as "the influence of an invisible presence that causes a peculiar alteration of consciousness" (CW 11, para. 6). Jung believed that a prerequisite to having a *numinous experience* was "a prior readiness to trust a transcendent power" (Samuels, Shorter & Plaut, 1986, p. 100).

Jung reports the case of a young woman who made a similar declaration of her intent to remain sober. She wrote eloquently complaining about the skeptical response of others to her intentions to remain sober and then blamed them for her drinking.

> The everlasting mistrust, the everlasting disbelief of these pessimists in the final moral cure, saps your strength and breaks your courage. You see yourself abandoned by others and finally you abandon yourself. Then you try to deaden your torments of soul and seize on any and every means that deadens—so long as there's spirit in it. Thank God I no longer need this deadening now. (CW 1, para. 200)

Six months later this same patient was "re-admitted to the Burghölzli for delirium tremens, having lately drunk methylated spirits and eau de cologne" (CW 1, para. 203).

Lois' response to Bill's determination to stop drinking clearly expresses the exasperation of spouses, partners, relatives, friends, and employers who are rightly cynical about an alcoholic's everlasting professions of intent to remain sober. Jung's patient expressed the self-righteous view of the alcoholic who may well use the lack of other's support as an excuse to drink. Both "sides" should understand that alcoholism cannot be cured by the person themselves, nor indeed by any human power. Paradoxically, while will-power is necessary, it is not the only ingredient that contributes to sobriety; the vital ingredient is, as stated in step two, "a Power greater than ourselves".

Step two is the beginning of rebirth and is symbolised appropriately by the Greek mythological god Dionysus who was "twice-born". He was the god of fecundity and wine. Reputedly he discovered wine and was an expert in tending the vines. Like the Jekyll and Hyde alcoholic he has a dual nature whereby he can bring joy and divine ecstasy, but is capable of erupting into brutal rages. It is said that if Dionysus chooses he can drive a person insane. Similarly, alcohol abuse can lead to Korsakov's psychosis.

Step three

Made a decision to turn our will and our lives over to the care of God as we understand him

Step three of the programme of A.A. is pivotal in the recovery process. It's about turning "our will", the ego, over to the care of the Self. Turning the will over is best exemplified in the first line of the prayer of St. Francis: *Lord, make me an instrument of Your peace.* In essence it is a struggle between the ego and the Self: in A.A. parlance, ego is an acronym for "Edging God Out". Not surprisingly people try to cling onto the notion of personal power and individual control and refuse to surrender their will, while others try to surrender their will and then the ego rears its head and takes it back. For most people in recovery it's an ongoing daily struggle between the ego and the Self.

John's story:

> Not sure I ever did step three completely, I try to remember in the morning to give gratitude and to say that Thine will be done but usually soon forget and it's my will that has to be done—I think to survive I do that but lately as I get older I see what it really means in that if I give over my will to God then I become his or her instrument and he or she can work through me to do good in the world. That now is my guiding philosophy and whenever I sense that happening, my life is happier than ever, indeed happy beyond my wildest dreams. But I still have "impure" thoughts and wonder if that is my will ousting God, can't imagine having "impure" thoughts and still being fully in tune with the divine grace of God? Still it is progress not perfection but I strive to do my best, as my wife says, never knew someone who tried so hard to be good but fails so miserably! (Personal interview, 15 August 2013)

Susan's story:

> It is so much easier to live trying my best to take the correct action but turning the outcome over to my Higher Power. For example, I have recently been attending job interviews and rather than conniving and manipulating the outcome I go, try my best and leave the rest up to my Higher Power. (*Share*, March 2013, p. 5)

Explanation

The first two steps act as a gentle introduction to a new life. In the first step the person with an alcohol problem admits their powerlessness over alcohol—simply it is more powerful than them—it has them beat! The second step is about accepting that there is a power in the universe that is greater than humans and it could help an alcoholic stop drinking and restore normality to their lives. If accepted, these first two steps combined can be the beginning of a new life. The third step is the first time that the word "God" is introduced and it is underlined that it is a God "as we understood Him." According to Bill, the effectiveness of the whole A.A. programme will rest upon how well and how earnestly "we have tried to come to a decision to turn our will and our lives over to the care of God *as we understood Him*" (Anon, 2002, p. 36).

Bill wrote that once having accepted that the troubles we encountered were "basically of our own making" (Anon, 1991a, p. 62), he advised recovering alcoholics to get down upon their knees and say,

> God, I offer myself to Thee—to build with me and to do with me as Thou wilt. Relieve me of the bondage of self, that I may better do Thy will. Take away my difficulties, that victory over them may bear witness to those I would help of Thy Power, Thy Love, and Thy Way of life. May I do Thy will always! (Anon, 1991a, p. 63)

A shortened version of this prayer is contained in the Lord's Prayer— "Thy will be done". In the Bible, there is also, "Father, if it is Your will, take this cup away from Me: nevertheless not My will, but Yours, be done" (Luke 22:42. Bible). Interestingly the word "cup" is interpreted to mean "burden" but in alcoholic terms the word "glass" could be substituted. People who abide by this prayer report a relief from the bondage that is entailed in focusing selfishly on oneself.

In this step the recovering person admits that the ego has until now been the director of their life. It has failed and brought them to a dark place. Their best thinking had brought them to a rock bottom and it is unlikely that their best thinking alone will get them out of it. So in desperation they are willing to try what seems to work for many others who were in their predicament.

Twelve Steps and Twelve Traditions (Anon, 2002) cites a version of the Buddhist maxim, "in defeat there is victory". "The more we become willing to depend on a Higher Power, the more independent we actually are" (Anon, 2002, p. 37). Dependence on a Higher Power is a healthy means of gaining true independence from the spirit of alcohol. There is nothing wrong with a healthy dependency; for example, we are dependent on electricity and it makes us more independent in our everyday lives.

Jungian perspective

From a Jungian perspective the third step introduces a person to their true Self. Paying heed to our true Self allows us to become the person we were born to be, to develop our potential to the maximum (Samuels, Shorter, & Plaut, 1986, p. 135). The third step is another incremental step in helping the ego to submit itself to the true Self. This involves acknowledging that the power of the Self is greater than the ego. The ego only has to submit, to be weakened, as opposed to be annihilated. The ego will continue to function and remain as "the centre of consciousness" (CW 12, para. 44), but will understand it is no longer the master and will begin to act more in the service of the Self.

John Sanford, Jungian analyst and Episcopalian priest, offers a clear understanding of the relationship between Self and the ego:

> In Jungian psychology there are two centres of the personality. The ego is the center of consciousness, whereas the Self is the center of the total personality ... While the ego is a self-contained little center of the circle contained within the whole, the Self can be understood as the greater circle. (Quoted in Zweig, 1991, p. 24)

Jung considered that the ego was very necessary to help us function in our external lives. It's as though when born the person is a whole Self and then the Self allows an ego to develop on the understanding that it is an emissary in the service of the Self. However, by the age of forty when the ego has fulfilled many of its functions in relation to forging a career and maybe procreating, a sense of mortality enters a person's consciousness. The question is asked what is life about? It is here the Self comes forward to answer that question. The person has a new purpose in the second half of life; it is to allow the emergence of the true Self to act as the guiding force in their lives. However, the ego feels powerful and does not want the humble Self to be the main personality, ego does not want to take a second position to the true Self. Indeed in some instances the ego would rather die than do so.

With alcoholics, this aggrandisement takes the form of excessive drinking as though to suppress the spirit of the Self. Hence Jung's axiom "spiritus contra spiritum" (see Appendix One), translates as "one spirit (alcohol) contradicts the Spirit".

Step four

Made a searching and fearless moral inventory of ourselves

John:

> Yes I wrote all the bad things I had done in my life and kept writing, then made the mistake of asking my wife did I have any defects of character that she could think of as I was out of stuff to write about—she looked at me aghast and was about to unleash a flood of my defects but I said it was alright and went back to writing and then the pen ran out of ink so I left it at that. What I did learn was how self centered I was and always thought I was in the right except with my wife to whom I found it easier to apologise even when I thought I was in the right, so that in itself is a good exercise! (Personal interview, 15 August 2013)

Stuart:

> Sponsor made it clear that I was to hold nothing back and to be unafraid and painstaking or I may well drink again … I wasn't entirely sure that I would divulge absolutely everything to myself (step four was the first time I had been honest to myself), my sponsor and Higher Power. There were certain facts about my life and behaviour I thought I would take to the grave. (*Share*, April 2013, pp. 5–6)

Evan:

> Basically we all suffer from the seven sins and as I wrote about myself, I began to realise although people hurt me, that I had played my part in the charade I called life. Power, fame, and a pat on the back; that's what I wanted deep down. Self-justification was my excuse about life and alcohol. Belief that because I worked, paid my bills, put food on the table, didn't hit my wife, that I wasn't hurting anybody, but how wrong I was! How I would justify to get a drink, I would justify walking off a job by blaming the boss or the shifts and life by saying nobody understood. (*Share*, April 2013, pp. 4–5)

Dave:

> My sponsor asked me to write my life story from my earliest thought ... as I wrote the defects became even more glaring; rebellion; sympathy; attention; wishful thinking; all brought depression and more excuses, total insanity. (*Share*, April 2013, pp. 4–5)

Explanation

The first three steps include admitting powerlessness over alcohol, coming to believe there is a power in the universe that is greater than humans and making a decision to turn "our lives over to the care of God as we understood Him". The first three steps are the foundations for step four. Step four entails actually putting pen to paper and writing out character defects at length. It is one of the fundamental steps that leads a person towards recognising their character defects. This is a daunting step for many people. So step four is usually approached with the guidance of a sponsor.

Making a moral inventory involves a vigorous and painstaking effort to discover defects of character. Doing the fourth step normally involves writing a list of these defects. Bill Wilson advises focusing on the seven deadly sins of wrath, greed, sloth, pride, lust, envy, and gluttony (Anon, 2002, p. 50). He suggests examining,

> Where our natural desires have warped us (and) to look squarely at the unhappiness this has caused others and ourselves. By discovering what our emotional deformities are, we can move towards their correction. (Ibid., p. 44)

Jungian perspective

Interestingly, Jung understands that when taking a moral inventory it is necessary to actually write down the details. He writes:

> It is very important to fix this whole procedure in writing at the time of its occurrence, for you then have ocular evidence that will effectively counteract the ever-ready tendency to self deception. A running commentary is absolutely necessary in dealing with the shadow, because otherwise its actuality cannot be fixed. Only in this painful way is it possible to gain a positive insight into the complex nature of one's personality. (CW 14, para. 706)

In Jungian terms, step four is comparable to confronting the shadow as part of the first stage of the individuation process. Jung understands that while it takes a great deal of conscious and moral effort to confront the shadow, it is necessary in order to become whole, "it is a therapeutic necessity, indeed, the first requisite of any thorough psychological method, for consciousness to confront its shadow" (CW 14, para. 514). Confronting the shadow refers to acknowledging the dark side of our nature which our ego tries to deny. Usually the dark side of our nature manifests as character faults. We learn to live with our faults usually by blindly refusing to acknowledge them even when to others they are staring us in the face. Instead we usually try to get rid of our faults by projecting them onto others; usually our nearest and dearest family members and work colleagues and especially authority figures. We always see our own faults best in others. An example is the person who is preoccupied with money but despises similar people and condemns them as money grabbers or misers. Jung explained that we tend to see our inferior shadow parts best in others so that if we are irritated by someone it can lead to an understanding of ourselves. He describes this as "expulsion of a subjective content into an object" or more specifically, "The subject gets rid of painful, incompatible contents by projecting them" (CW 6, para. 783). Similarly, in A.A. there is an adage that when you point a finger at another you are also pointing three fingers at yourself. The programme of A.A. teaches that if you are disturbed by anyone then the trouble is within yourself.

In Jungian analysis the difficulties associated with acknowledging our shadow side are generally gently guided by the analyst, whilst in the programme of A.A. a person taking the fourth step may then go on in the fifth step to tell their defects of character and past misdeeds to their sponsor or trusted confidante.

Jung writes of confronting the shadow,

> Man stands forth as he really is and shows what was hidden under the mask of conventional adaptation; the shadow. This is now raised to consciousness and integrated with the ego which means a move in the direction of wholeness. Wholeness is not so much perfection as completeness. (CW 16, para. 452)

Similarly in A.A. there is a popular phrase "Progress rather than perfection". Jung is careful to write that confronting the shadow is a move in the direction of wholeness and that more work still has to be done. Step four is the beginning of the ego accepting that it is not all good. There is an adage in A.A. that states, "That in the best of us, there is the worst and in the worst of us, there is the best". This is a reminder to everyone that we are all part of the imperfect human condition. Similarly Jung reminds us that:

> Assimilation of the shadow gives a man body so to speak; the animal sphere of instinct, as well as the primitive or archaic psyche, emerge into the zone of consciousness and can no longer be repressed by fictions and illusions. In this way, man becomes for himself the difficult problem he really is. He must always remain conscious of the fact that he is such a problem if he wants to develop at all. (CW 16, para. 452)

According to Jung, "Once the naked truth has been revealed the discussion can get down to essentials; ego and shadow are no longer divided but are brought together in an—admittedly precarious—unity" (CW 16, para. 452). Being conscious of our own darkness has the benefits that it helps us cope better with the darkness of "others". Indeed, facing the shadow and the insight it gives can help individuals, communities and even nation states gain a greater understanding of their unconscious complexes. Jung writes:

> If people can be educated to see the lowly side of their own natures, it may be hoped that they will also learn to understand and to love their fellow men better. A little less hypocrisy and a little more tolerance towards oneself can only have good results in respect for

our neighbour; for we are all too prone to transfer to our fellows the injustice and violence we inflict upon our own natures. (CW 7, para. 439)

The writing out of character defects gently prepares the groundwork for the next step, which is confessional in nature because it asks the person to admit their wrongs to another human being.

Step five

Admitted to God, to ourselves, and to another human being the exact nature of our wrongs

Jack:

> I chose the person to hear my step five carefully and decided upon a local Baptist minister. This man and his family had chosen to adopt two severely disabled children. This was a massive commitment and something I knew I would never contemplate. A true example of 'walking the walk'. The minister invited me to spend the evening at his house, where I admitted to him the exact nature of my wrongs. I don't know exactly how long I was there but I remember walking home at about 10pm in bright sunlight. (*Share*, May 2013, p. 9)

John:

> I took the program quite seriously and went to visit Fr. Anthony a renowned fifth step priest in a monastery in Tipperary. I had been in psychoanalysis for five years and had already gone over my secrets and shames many times and honestly this was not that much different. We spoke for about three hours and it was helpful in that I had fulfilled a serious condition of getting sober. Looking back I realise how arrogant I was in that I just appeared at the monastery to stay the night and expected to see Fr. Anthony without an appointment. My God, the arrogance! But now aware of that defect, I have turned it around and the experience has served me well in that whenever someone wants to see me urgently, knocks on my door without an appointment or phones me late at night, I don't stand on my high horse but instead remember the humanity that was shown to me.

> Then I heard there was another Fr. Anthony in Carlow and I wondered had I spoken to the wrong one? So off I went to see him just to make sure. From both men I realised that they had something special, they had completed their journey and you meet few men like them, the type that radiate a warm nature, what I would now call a spiritual glow. (Personal interview, 15 August 2013)

The relief felt by the many who intended on taking their secrets to the grave is professed by many others who changed their minds and decided to unburden themselves. For example, Brian recounts his experience as follows: "I can honestly say that doing steps four and five was the best and greatest thing I have ever done in my life, and it was dependent on me coming to A.A. and getting a sponsor" (*Share*, May 2013, p. 7).

Explanation

Step five helps alcoholics to face reality by confessing their innermost secrets to another human being. Usually a person chooses their sponsor to confide in. In turn their sponsor will tell their sponsee about their own character defects and escapades so as to encourage a mutual sharing of secret transgressions. However, sometimes people choose someone outside of the fellowship, usually a worldly wise, compassionate, and non-judgemental person. Not surprisingly, a popular choice is a priest, rabbi, therapist, or pastoral counsellor.

Twelve Steps and Twelve Traditions states that step five will bring a sense of humility and is defined as "a clear recognition of what and who we really are, followed by a sincere attempt to become what we could be" (Anon, 2002, p. 59). By becoming "what and who we really are," recovering alcoholics can also be of maximum service to their fellow citizens.

According to Bill Wilson, "When it comes to ego deflation, few steps are harder to take than five", the advice is that in order to get rid of "the tormenting demons", it is necessary to talk to someone about these defects. The practice of admitting defects of character to someone is an ancient practice and has "been validated in every century, and it characterises the lives of all spiritually centered and truly religious people" (Anon, 2002, p. 57).

A common statement that many people in recovery make is that they remember acts that are so shocking they fear telling any right-minded person for fear of rejection. However, usually the sponsor is able to top any story they hear. Not sharing the whole truth or holding back can be catastrophic. The Big Book advises,

> Time after time newcomers have tried to keep to themselves certain facts about their lives. Trying to avoid this humbling experience, they have turned to easier methods. Almost invariably they got drunk ... they had not learned enough of humility, fearlessness and honesty, in the sense we find it necessary, until they told someone else *all* their life story. (Anon, 1991a, pp. 72–73)

The Big Book cites the benefits of doing step five:

> Once we have taken this step, withholding nothing, we are delighted. We can look the world in the eye. We can be alone at perfect peace and ease. Our fears fall from us. We begin to feel the nearness of our creator. We may have had certain spiritual beliefs, but now we begin to have a spiritual experience. The feeling that the drink problem has disappeared will often come strongly. We feel we are on the Broad Highway walking hand in hand with the Spirit of the Universe. (Anon, 1991a, p. 75)

For the person completing the fifth step the effect of telling another person their darkest secrets is cathartic. Bill writes that, "Many in A.A., once agnostic or atheist, tells us that it was during this stage of step five that he first actually felt the presence of God" (Anon, 2002, p. 63).

Jungian perspective

The *Oxford English Dictionary* (2014) includes the following example as a definition of "confession": "An acknowledgement that one has done something about which one is ashamed or embarrassed". The emphasis is on the need for acknowledgment to oneself.

In relation to alcoholism, this acknowledgement to oneself helps quash denial which is a symptom of alcoholism. In Jungian terms the confessional aspect of step five helps the recovering person to develop their personality to its full capacity. That development includes them getting in touch with their true Self. Jungian analysis, like most psychotherapies, involves a person building up a trust with their therapists and eventually confessing their innermost secrets. The benefit that comes from admitting our secrets to another human being is that we no longer feel isolated and we can begin to feel part of society rather than apart from it. In Jungian terms confronting the shadow, or assimilating the aspects of our ego that we wish to deny, brings us more into reality with our true Selves.

Jung was conscious of the dangers of secrets and the benefits of sharing them. He viewed secrets as acting like "psychic poison that alienates their possessor from the community" (CW 16, para. 124), but there is a cure: "A secret shared with several persons is as beneficial as a merely private secret is destructive. The latter works like a burden of guilt, cutting off the unfortunate possessor from communion with his fellows" (CW 16, para. 125). Sharing secrets in therapy or at meetings of A.A. can relieve the burden of guilt.

Members of A.A. who have taken a fifth step with a sponsor or Pastor usually report a tremendous feeling of relief. According to Bill Wilson following a fifth step, "We may have had certain spiritual beliefs, but now we begin to have a spiritual experience" (Anon, 1991a, p. 75). In analysis, the client is able to use the analyst as a confessor; similarly in A.A. the person in recovery may use a sponsor who will help end their sense of isolation. Jung views the confessional as similar to the "first beginnings of all analytical treatment" (CW 16, para. 123; see also Todd, 1985, p. 46).

Sponsors are the epitome of the archetypal wounded healer. Kerenyi, a colleague of Jung who elucidated on the archetype of the wounded healer, describes them as having the capacity "to be at home in the darkness of suffering and there to find germs of light and recovery with which, as though by enchantment, to bring forth Asclepius, the sun like healer" (woundedhealer.net, 2014). Jung explained the concept of the wounded healer: "It is his own hurt that gives the measure of his power to heal. This, and nothing else, is the meaning of the Greek myth of the wounded physician" (CW 16, para. 239).

Similarly, in analytical psychology, often the analyst as the guide may themselves be wounded healers. A.A. sponsors will have experienced the vagaries of alcoholism and normally be naturally empathetic. There is an archetypal element in passing on knowledge from the initiated to the mentor. As with many crafts and fraternities, the new entrant has to become an apprentice to a master. For example, new initiates into Freemasonry have to find a "Master and from him gain instruction" (Lomas, 2010, p. 13).

Jung describes the confrontation with the shadow as the "apprentice piece in the individual's development" (CW 9i, para. 61). By this, he means that it is the starting point of the individuals' individuation process. He further states that, "The integration of the shadow or the realisation of the personal unconscious marks the first stage in the analytical process and without it recognition of the anima and animus is impossible" (CW9ii, para. 42). Translated to A.A., and therapy in general, this means getting in touch with our feelings, through which we can get in touch with our true Self.

Step six

Were entirely ready to have God remove all these defects of character

John:

> Must admit didn't pay too much attention to this step—thought my main defect of character was my big ego, my self interest and really just couldn't ever see those ingrained defects ever going away. Thought maybe I needed my defects such as selfishness to survive in order to make my way in the world. But I did continue to pray that my defects of character would be removed without knowing quite what they were. Just being honest! So as I continue in the program, I try more and more to focus on trying to be of service to other people and A.A. advises that the less we think of ourselves and the more we think of others, constant thought of others, then the happier we will be. I find this is absolutely true and as I grow older, I feel an urge to do good and do more good—indeed I think it will be a sin if my life is just about leaving my money to my well off adult children. I am beginning to think that maybe my maker has given me comparatively good financial and intellectual resources and I must put these to the very best use for humanity. Coming to understand that the programme is about becoming of

maximum service to God and my fellows. (Personal interview, 15 August 2013)

Niamh:

Before I joined the fellowship of Alcoholics Anonymous, I had no idea what a character defect was, and it took me 18 months to realise that I even had them! ... At first I couldn't cope with the term "character defect" and preferred to refer to them as my "*index of maladjustments.*" My natural default setting is one of self loathing and shame, so the thought that I was full of these "defects" was almost too hard to bear. But by taking a deep breath and opening up to do step five progressing on to step six, I see that I am not alone in my defects—everybody appears to have them!—When I commenced step six I had no idea what a difficult but amazing step it would be ... . I saw that facing these defects was just a way of simply trying to become a better person, and the result would be humility. (*Share*, June 2013, pp. 6–7)

Simon:

I calculated that I had fourteen defects of character namely, "Pride; Self-pity; Self-centeredness; Dishonesty; Arrogance; Envy; Jealousy; Lust; Intolerance; impatience; Selfishness; Jealousy; Sloth and Gluttony" .... The Big Book says on page 64; "our liquor was but a symptom. So we had to get down to causes and conditions." I now appreciate that the "causes and conditions," are the defects of character, which lead to resentment, something that can actually destroy us. (*Share*, June 2013, p. 9)

Eunice:

When I did my steps four and five with a sponsor, I was under the impression that all of these character defects belonged to the old drinking Eunice, rather than the new improved sober Eunice. I would probably have admitted out loud that I still wasn't perfect—but inside thinking that I wasn't far off. So when it came to doing the paperwork for step six, I didn't think that there would be too much to do—I was wrong. (*Share*, June 2013, pp. 5–6)

Explanation

By working steps one to five the recovering alcoholic has laid the firm foundation for the removal of their defects of character, especially by leading a life that is no longer lived on self-will "run riot". The defects that the alcoholic is attempting to be relieved of can be summarised in the seven deadly sins of pride, covetousness, lust, anger, gluttony, envy, and sloth.

The words of step six "entirely ready to have God remove all these defects of character", does not mean that all character defects will be taken away as the compulsion to drink was. The words "entirely ready" emphasises the fact that this step does not deal in half measures nor is it *a la carte*. It means there is a readiness to have all defects of character removed, even the favourite ones such as anger or pride. People in recovery do admit that they prefer to hang on to *some* of their defects. This may be because the ego never quite surrenders or dies until the last gasp of air leaves the body. Step six is never perfected and the ego will still be alive and kicking. According to Bill Wilson, "No matter how far we have progressed, desires will always be found which oppose the grace of God" (Anon, 2002, p. 67). In reality removal of defects of character will take time so the person in recovery may have to be content with gradual improvement. Undertaking the programme to this stage will have laid the ground for the deflation of the ego and the acquisition of some degree of humility. A degree of humbleness is a prerequisite for the taking of step six.

Twelve Steps and Twelve Traditions quotes a clergyman who says that step six, "separates the men from the boys" (Anon, 2002, p. 64). It is intended to prepare the alcoholic working the programme for the fact that this is a most difficult step. It involves reaffirming step three of turning "our will and our lives over to the care of God". In a way it is handing over the ego to the true Self. It is a Faustian pact in reverse, whereby the true Self is regained.

Jungian perspective

The sixth step is a time for reflection. Being entirely ready to have God remove all defects of character is also about preparing for the release of feelings. The steps gradually introduce the recovering person to their true Self and opens them to their innermost feelings. Feelings that may have been suppressed for years, feelings of both joy and anger.

Jung believed that the suppressed feelings of the male could be reawakened through the anima (feminine nature) in the male psyche. Similarly the suppressed thinking function of the female could be brought more to the fore through the animus (masculine nature) in the female psyche. When working the twelve steps, an unconscious contrasexual element may emerge, not in an obvious change of sexuality, but in a change related to the emergence of feelings in the male and *logos* in the female. Essentially, the person whether male or female matures emotionally and cognitively.

Jung believed that when as part of the individuation process, the soul begins to emerge, it has a feminine character (anima) in the man and in the woman a masculine character (animus) (CW 16, para. 522). Jung wrote "when the anima is strongly constellated, she softens the man's character and makes him touchy, irritable, moody, jealous, vain, and unadjusted" (CW 9i, para. 144).

Additionally, if as it happens, the feeling function has been suppressed in the male it can emerge, usually in mid-life or even later life in the form of an anima infatuation or through an obsession or infatuation: Jung gives as an example, "When a highly esteemed professor in his seventies abandons his family and runs off with a young red-headed actress ..." (CW 9i, para. 62).

In a woman, the animus may make the woman more dominant and logical and become more her own person, rather than the "wife of, daughter of or mother of". Jung views the animus in a woman as corresponding to the paternal *Logos*. Essentially, during the individuation process, the male becomes more in touch with their feeling function whilst the female allows her thinking function to come to the fore.

In therapeutic work there is an acknowledgement that for change to come about it normally has to be linked to feelings. So similarly in terms of alcohol recovery, there has to be not only a want but also a feeling of desire for sobriety.

Step seven

Humbly asked Him to remove our shortcomings

Andy:

> Step seven suggests we humbly ask God to remove our shortcomings. Nowhere in the Big Book does it say that they

will then be instantly removed. The point, I think is that we are willing to ask. In asking to be rid of my defects, I am trying to become a better person. But being human, I will always remain a long way from perfect. Those old defects will keep cropping up I reckon, just so long as I remain alive and human. (*Share*, July 2012, p. 11)

Maurice:

In rehab I was given a number of suggestions on how to do step seven but the main points that kept coming up were that I needed to find somewhere quiet and somewhere I felt close to my Higher Power. I never feel much closer to my Higher Power than when I am close to nature. So I chose to do mine down on the beach. (*Share*, July 2013, p. 4)

John:

Have to admit never quite understood this step. Perhaps being arrogant, feel that now I have reached this stage my shortcomings are fewer but then I remember my arrogance—yes have to admit my lack of patience when in a queue, have asked people ahead to hurry up much to the consternation of my wife, so yes I forget that I have shortcomings and indeed since I am not perfect will always have them! (Personal interview, 15 August 2013)

Tom:

In step seven I humbly ask for my shortcomings to be removed. I am unfinished business, a work in progress. My first thoughts each morning are no longer only of myself. The joy of helping others is beyond any fleeting pleasure gained from alcohol.

At my first meeting in London, they said "Let us love you until you can learn to love yourself."

If I am self obsessed I can't pass on the great way of life I have been given. (Personal interview, 12 March 2015)

Explanation

We might ask why the word is humbly used in this step. The answer, according to Bill Wilson is "For without some degree of humility, no alcoholic can stay sober at all" (Anon, 2002, p. 71). "Humble" is derived from the Latin word "humilis" meaning "low". It is defined as being "conscious of one's failings: modest and unpretentious; ordinary or not very important" (*Collins English Dictionary*, 2011).

When an alcoholic admits in the first step their powerlessness over alcohol, this in itself is a "humble admission of powerlessness" (Anon, 2002, p. 74). Once this admission is made it is a move toward "liberation from the paralysing grip" of alcohol (Ibid.). Crossing the threshold of an A.A. meeting for the first time is a humbling experience. Before crossing the parapet of A.A. most alcoholics considered themselves to be masters of the universe—now their sanity is reliant on attending a meeting in a basement church hall amongst people they once thought were the dregs of society. In attending the meeting they were prepared to meet the worst of characters but instead they meet captains of industry, famous film stars, rock musicians and yes some "down and outs" but mostly they meet ordinary people just like themselves! Indeed a motley bunch of people. Members are rarely interested in a person's status; it is their spiritual development that they value rather than the size of their bank account.

Step seven is linked to the previous three steps, whereby a searching and fearless moral inventory was made, the exact nature of wrongs were admitted and there was a whole-hearted willingness to have God remove all defects of character. Now in step seven there is a readiness to ask humbly to have shortcomings removed. This is the step where a selfish attitude is changed and a move is made away from preoccupation with self toward a greater interest in others. This is the beginning of preparing to be of maximum service to others and is one of the main aims of the programme of A.A. It is a rewarding move and the Big Book mentions that happiness resides not in thinking of self but in constant thought of others.

It is understood that learning humility may take time since generally most people with alcohol problems are self-centred and will not change overnight. When ready, they may be prepared to say the following prayer:

> My Creator, I am now willing that you should have all of me, good and bad. I pray that you now remove from me every single defect of character which stands in the way of my usefulness to you and my fellows. Grant me strength, as I go out from here, to do your bidding. Amen. (Anon, 1991, p. 76)

Jungian perspective

The world's great religions are united on the sacredness of the three fundamental virtues, charity, truthfulness, and humility: James 4:10 refers to humility, "Humble yourselves in the sight of the Lord, and he shall lift you up". This is what happens at A.A. meetings when recovering alcoholics admit their character defects. The Koran states, "Verily, those who believe and do righteous good deeds, and humble themselves before their Lord, they will be dwellers of Paradise to dwell therein forever" (11:23). Doing righteous good deeds should come naturally when having completed the programme of A.A. Humility is associated with one of Judaism's most outstanding representatives: No one was ever as humble as Moses (Roth, 1973).

The alchemists teach us that in order to be worthy of finding the philosopher's stone, the appropriate piety must be developed (Melville, 2002, p. 10). Jung advised therapists, "Let no day pass without humbly remembering that everything has still to be learned" (cited in Sclater, 1993, p. 14).

Jungians might differ with the seventh step believing that character shortcomings are part of our shadow and should be assimilated and modified rather than completely removed. This would mean that the Self would assimilate the shadow part of our nature, good and bad, and accept this state as being part of the human condition. Similarly, it might appear that there is a contradiction between step seven and asking "Him to remove our shortcomings" and the Big Book, which promises, "We will not regret the past nor wish to shut the door on it" (Anon, 1991a, p. 83). But the words "humbly asked" provide the key. It is a reminder that our shortcomings may be revisited upon us if we return to a state of arrogance. We may no longer act as arrogantly but we still retain the memories of our conceit. Jung quotes from a sixteenth-century alchemical treatise, *The Rosary of the Philosophers* which also makes the point that we should not regret the past that brought us to our downfall. Indeed Jung considers the mistakes of the past to be a jewel that brings us into analysis, self-reflection or recovery. He writes: "despise not the ash, for it is the diadem of thy heart, and the ash of things that endure" (CW 13, para. 183).

According to the Big Book, the memories of the past may become an asset because they help the person in recovery to relate to others struggling with the problem. Memories of the past remain as a reminder that they are living proof that positive change is possible. It is probable that in the same way we need to know darkness to understand light, the alcoholic needs to experience the dark shadow side of their nature, in order to appreciate their opposite nature, that is, spirituality. Jung believed that "without the experience of the opposites there is no experience of wholeness. ... For this reason Christianity rightly insists on sinfulness and original sin" (CW 12, para. 24).

Step eight

Made a list of all persons we had harmed, and became willing to make amends to them all

Ronny:

> The first part of step eight was relatively easy, although I missed several people off my list the first time round. ... Then comes the second part of step eight, became willing to make amends to them all! I had a particular problem with one person who I thought had harmed ME more. My sponsor suggested that I try to look at the problem in a different way; so I forgave myself for feeling that way and agreed that I would, if the opportunity arose, make amends to that person in case I had upset them. Some twelve years later, I haven't had to test this as I haven't met them again! Time has made me even more willing to do so if the occasion arises as the reasons behind it all are, with hindsight, trivial. Beer glasses do tend to magnify problems, don't they? I understood that part of cleaning house was clearing up any problems I had created or caused with other people or if I had hurt or insulted anyone." (*Share*, net. 2013)

John:

> Well again, was little offended by the presumptuousness of this step—how did they know I had harmed people. Never thought of it like that but then I began to wonder—well there was my wife, she seemed to accept my drinking. But having attended a couple of Al Anon meetings I wonder if I take control too much—many of the women at Al Anon spoke about their low self esteem, as exemplified by their reluctance to buy new clothes for themselves—usually bought stuff in the second hand shop.

My wife just wasn't interested in buying clothes. So I asked her about it and she said that once when she bought something I criticised it harshly and that put her off buying clothes and then said whenever she liked something she knew I would dislike it and whenever I liked something she would dislike it—perhaps very symbolic but we still manage to get along. But after hearing the other side at the Al Anon meeting I feel crushed at the thought that I may have affected her confidence and self esteem. Other people I had harmed—often say I would hate to have someone like me work for me, so many jobs and so many arguments that I have to admit I must have been wrong some of the time at least if not most of the time! (Personal interview, 15 August 2013)

Explanation

A booklet titled *The Golden Book of Action* by Father John Doe (1950), advises that when an alcoholic has a problem they shouldn't start analysing "worrying and debating" and constantly thinking about it, instead they should simply take action and do something. Step eight is a gentle introduction to making amends. It builds on step four, when a fearless moral inventory was made; then in step five defects of character were admitted to another human being. Step six involved a readiness to have God remove all these defects and in step seven; God was asked to humbly remove shortcomings. Step eight only asks that there be a willingness to make amends, not that the amends be made, yet. So step eight asks for a willingness to make amends to all persons who may have been harmed. This may include spouses, partners, family, friends, and employers. Making amends may be straightforward, for example, repaying stolen money. It can be more subtle, for example, if a person's good name has been defamed, then whatever can be done to restore it, must be done. The Big Book gives an example of this when a man confesses publicly about ruinously slandering another man (Anon, 1991a, p. 80). Just as the twelve step programme requires a strong appreciation of the nature of the wrongs done and to whom they were done, a true confession also requires acceptance of personal responsibility and a willingness to right those wrongs. This is the reason why in Catholic confession there is no absolution without contrition.

Jungian perspective

In the Catholic religion, confession is a regular custom and part of the confessional entails a penance which is a form of making amends. Furthermore before the penitent can be absolved they are required to be sincere about making amends. They must be at least willing to try and change their behaviour, so as not to repeat the transgression. Jung considered that Catholics, because they have this facility of confession, were not in need of analysis as much as Protestants were (Jung, 1975, pp. 75–76).

Jung believed that, "To cherish secrets and hold back emotion is a psychic misdemeanour for which nature finally visits us with sickness" (CW 16, para. 132). Jung believed that the only way to get rid of this sickness is through the reconciliation with one's self that follows a successful confession. Elizabeth Todd, who has studied confession and forgiveness from a Jungian perspective, writes that a successful confession entails making some sort of amends. "When Jung is speaking of confession, he is referring to a ritual which has two parts: the need to confess and the need to be forgiven and reconciled" (Todd, 1985, p. 41). According to Todd, it is only when the process of confession and forgiveness have been accomplished that the penitent is "able to feel restored and reconciled in the community" (Ibid., p. 46).

Making amends involves more than simply apologising, it involves, wherever possible, an attempt at restitution. A direct approach may be necessary. For example, if money has been stolen or embezzled then every effort should be made to return it. Making direct amends to the person rather than through a mediator, such as a priest, is a courageous act and relates to the teachings of the early Gnostics. They communed directly to God, as similarly recovering alcoholics now confess directly to the person they have harmed. In practice what is achieved by confession is the reconciliation of the ego with the true Self. Similarly, in the individuation process, integration of the various parts of the person includes acceptance and forgiveness of the shadow part of the ego.

Step nine

*Made direct amends to such people wherever possible,
except when to do so would injure them or others*

Denis, as advised by his sponsor, went to see the people on his list, which included family and former managers.

Once I started doing it, I found it a delight. People only wanted the best for me. When I met people, I had a great response. All my family members were glad that I had happily, healthily, and spiritually changed my life. They only wanted to see me happy and well. (*Share*, September 2013, p. 9)

John:

As I said I didn't feel that I had hurt people so no real amends to make—but you know looking back at the relationship with my mother—could have been different—everyone agrees she was mad but I could have been more civil—sent her a solicitors letter to keep away—sad reflecting back but she was upsetting the children with her mind games and madness. Still I should been more composed, in retrospect could have handled it more serenely if I had worked the steps? (Personal interview, 15 August 2013)

Ryan:

I approached my sister ... but I wasn't expecting what I got at all. "You are certainly not an alcoholic" she roared down the phone. "You weren't brought up to be an alcoholic, your parents weren't alcoholic and I deny anything else you say on the matter." I was left in a state of shock when I put the phone down. I rang my sponsor who advised not to say anything else on the matter to her and keep off the subject. (*Share*, September 2013, p. 4)

Explanation

While step eight involves writing out a list of all people who have been harmed, step nine then encourages attempts to make amends to the people on the list. The previous four steps have been a gradual build up to this difficult action. Even with the steady build up this is still a difficult step for many people.

The Big Book advises that discretion be exercised when making amends. As Ryan's story illustrates, amends may not always be accepted and discretion has to be used. *Twelve Steps and Twelve Traditions* advises, "Good judgment, a careful sense of timing, courage, and prudence—these are the qualities we shall need when we take step nine" (Anon, 2002, p. 85). Yet, many people report that when they approached former friends, ex-wives, past employers, that their amends were accepted amicably and indeed the recipients were pleasantly surprised that they were making something good out of their life.

Jungian perspective

Jung is emphatic that for confession to be successful,

> A general and merely academic "insight into one's mistakes" is ineffectual, for then the mistakes are not really seen at all, only the idea of them. But they show up acutely when a human relationship brings them to the fore and when they are noticed by the other person as well as by oneself. Then and then only can they really be felt and their true nature recognised. Similarly, confessions made to one's secret self generally have little or no effects whereas confessions made to another are much more promising. (CW 16, para. 503)

Jung's understanding of confession as above accords with the steps of A.A. in that a true confession must be not only to ourselves, but to God and another human being.

The purpose of making amends based on A.A. principles has a dual intention; it entails restitution and hopefully making recipients feel better. Additionally, according to the Big Book, "Our real purpose is to fit ourselves to be of maximum service to God and the people about us" (Anon, 1991a, p. 77). Completing step nine means the difficult work is nearly over and the promises of A.A. begin to come into fruition in particular that, "We are going to know a new freedom and a new happiness".

The remaining promises contained in the Big Book begin to happen (see Appendix Four). This is because working the nine steps has healed the alcoholic's mind to the extent that, as in individuation, "There comes into being a higher point of view where both conscious and unconscious are represented" (CW 16, para. 479). This meeting of consciousness with the unconscious may not be obvious, but it appears in the recovering person's life as stated in the Promises of A.A., "We will intuitively know how to handle situations which used to baffle us" (Anon, 1991a, p. 84). So that, "What used to be the hunch or occasional inspiration gradually becomes a working part of the mind" (Anon,

1991a, p. 87). Indeed it may be other people who notice the recovering person's new-found harmony and wisdom that comes from their conscious contact with their Higher Power.

Step ten

Continued to take personal inventory and when we were wrong promptly admitted it

Peter:

> This is the step that keeps my programme fresh and me living in the day, the idea that I will be wrong meant that I don't have to be perfect. This takes the pressure off me. I'm the type of person if I can't be the best at something I jack it in. This step keeps me human and right size. I realised that I get back what I give out. If I'm angry I meet a lot of angry people, if I'm driving like an idiot I meet a lot of stupid drivers on the road. (*Share*, October 2013, p. 8)

John:

> Ok! so am doing this back to front in that I now take a personal inventory and look to where I may have done wrong and now recognise the narcissism in me and indeed in other fellow alcoholics—it's not a pathological narcissism, more due to a lack of parental attention as a child and trying to compensate for that now by getting attention and above all expecting to get my way as a matter of course and as I get older fewer and fewer people respond to that attitude so I try now to be a little humble sometimes and accept that life is not fair indeed if it were I would not be in the privilege place I am in, indeed would not be living a life beyond my wildest dreams! (Personal interview, 15 August 2013)

Explanation

By the time step ten is reached sanity has returned and "we have now cleaned up the past and ceased fighting anything or anyone" (Anon, 1991a, p. 84). However there is no cure for alcoholism, "What we really have is a daily reprieve contingent on the maintenance of our spiritual condition" (Anon, 1991a, p. 85).

In the Big Book, Bill Wilson writes that by the time step ten is reached the recovering person may be fortunate enough to have achieved balance in their dealings with the world: "We are neither cocky, nor are we afraid. That is our experience. That is how we react so long as we keep in fit spiritual condition" (Anon, 1991a, p. 85).

Twelve Steps and Twelve Traditions offers general advice that helps people in recovery cope with daily irritants. Perhaps the major danger to sobriety is the harbouring of resentments, "Few people have been more victimised by resentments than have we alcoholics" (Anon, 2002, p. 92). The word resentment is derived from the Latin word "*senitire*" to feel and "*resentire*" means to re-feel past hurts. Resentment is defined as the re-send-ing or revisiting of old wounds, so people in recovery are advised not to open up old conflicts. It is likened to a person continually scratching a scab to ensure it remains unhealed. More graphically, deliberately rekindling a resentment about a person is compared to drinking a poison and hoping the resented person will die! Similarly, A.A. advises that anger is better left to people who can handle it. Even if provoked to respond in anger, there is the reminder that, "Nothing pays off like restraint of tongue and pen" (Ibid., p. 93). But above all A.A. urges tolerance. When in doubt about actions towards others there is the reminder to pause and say, "Thy will (not mine) be done" (Anon, 1991a, p. 85). At night the person in recovery may reflect on their day and "thank God for the blessings we have received and sleep in good conscience" (Anon, 2002, p. 97).

The Big Book reminds the recovering person that when they reach step ten, "To some extent we have become God-conscious" (Anon, 1991a, p. 85). However, far from suggesting that the recovering person rests on their laurels they are instead advised about progressing to the next step to improve their conscious contact with God.

Jungian perspective

By the time step ten is reached the person in recovery has put into practice the main points of the A.A. programme which are "acceptance of our faults, confession and forgiveness of ourselves and others" (Anon, 1991a, p. 85). From here on in they are implementing the changes that they have brought upon ourselves and, "It will become more and more evident as we go forward that it is pointless to become angry or to get hurt by people who, like us, are suffering from the pains of growing up" (Anon, 2002, pp. 94–95).

Recovering alcoholics realise that others are similar to themselves and are on the divine human journey. This is also the essence of Jungian individuation—that we are all interconnected described as "Unus Mundus", connected via a divine being. Jung advises therapists that they are

> Not just working for this particular patient, who may be quite insignificant, but for himself as well and his own soul, and in doing so he is perhaps laying an infinitesimal grain in the scales of humanity's soul. Small and invisible as this contribution may be, it is yet an *opus magnum* ... The ultimate questions of psychotherapy are not a private matter—they represent a supreme responsibility. (CW 16, para. 449)

Jung is referring to the advancement of mankind's consciousness. The recovering alcoholic is a part of this advancement, always striving to improve an otherwise base nature, enlighten their consciousness and progress morally and spiritually.

Step eleven

Sought through prayer and meditation to improve our conscious contact with God as we understood Him, praying only for knowledge of His will for us and the power to carry that out

Catherine:

> I never expected this when I first came into the Fellowship .... In step three I made a decision to turn my will and my life over to the care of my Higher Power, but in this step, I really get to see the fruits of that decision. For me step eleven is the epitome of the slogan "Let Go and Let God", and for that I am truly grateful. (*Share*, November 2013, p. 5)

John:

> Definitely this has had a huge impact on my life. Fortunate to be introduced to Buddhist meditation. For me meditation is like a meeting, it allows a new energy to improve my attitude. If I have a problem, I will go to a meeting and my attitude to the problem will

change and lessen, similarly when I go to my meditation group, I leave with a different attitude basically, both meditation and meetings put things into perspective for me. (Personal interview, 15 August 2013)

Explanation

Step eleven is linked to the previous step because there is a "direct linkage among self-examination, meditation and prayer" (Anon, 2002, p. 100). Following step ten Bill writes, "If we have carefully followed directions, we have begun to sense the flow of His Spirit into us. To some extent we have become God-conscious. We have begun to develop this vital sixth sense" (Anon, 1991a, p. 85). This sixth sense is difficult to define, though according to *Twelve Steps and Twelve Traditions,* by the time step eleven is reached, there is a greater acceptance of "the conviction that God *does* 'move in a mysterious way His wonders to perform'" (Anon, 2002, p. 107).

St. Francis is held up as someone to emulate. He had been through the "emotional wringer" and reputedly wrote a prayer of how he wanted to be:

> Lord, make me an instrument of Thy peace;
> Where there is hatred, let me sow love;
> Where there is injury, pardon;
> Where there is error, truth;
> Where there is doubt, faith;
> Where there is despair, hope;
> Where there is darkness, light;
> And where there is sadness, joy.
> O Divine Master, Grant that I may not so much seek
> To be consoled as to console;
> To be understood as to understand;
> To be loved as to love.
> For it is in giving that we receive;
> It is in pardoning that we are pardoned;
> And it is in dying that we are born to eternal life. Amen
> (Anon 2002, pp. 101–102; for the origins of this prayer see americancatholic.org).

The essence of this prayer is that it is by unselfish, self-forgetting that we find our real Self. *Twelve Steps and Twelve Traditions* suggests that, "as beginners in meditation, we might now reread this prayer several times very slowly, savouring every word and trying to take in the deep meaning of each phrase and idea" (Anon, 2002, p. 102). Bill Wilson advocates meditation because "one of its major fruits is emotional balance" (Ibid., p. 104). Wilson also emphasised that the object of meditation is "to improve our conscious contact with God" (Ibid.)—in Jungian terms, conscious contact with the Self.

Jungian perspective

The twelve-step programme is quite clear in recommending prayer and meditation for improving conscious contact with God. By contrast Jung was apparently critical of Eastern philosophies, including meditation. Referring to meditation as an exercise developed "under Indian influence" he thought such methods as meditation "are of value only for increasing concentration and consolidating consciousness, but has no significance as regards affecting a synthesis of the personality. On the contrary, their purpose is to shield consciousness from the unconscious and to suppress it" (CW 14, para. 708). Here Jung and Bill Wilson apparently hold opposite views about using meditation to increase our conscious contact with our personal God. There is no doubt that given the proven benefits of meditation, Jung was perhaps too wary and elitist about the practice of meditation. He seems to have ignored the early experience of the Christian Church which favoured meditation and venerated those who practiced it, such as the Celtic monks of Glendalough, Clonmacnoise in Ireland and Iona in Scotland.[1]

Carl Jung and Bill Wilson have written that words without action are worthless: A saying attributed to Jung is: "You are what you do, *not* what you say you'll do" (goodreads.com/quotes/3240) Similarly, Wilson wrote "Now we need more action, without which we find that 'Faith without works is dead'" (Anon, 1991a, p. 76). Both men are here echoing the Biblical way of expressing this maxim: "What [doth it] profit, my brethren, though a man say he hath faith, and have not works? Can faith save him?" (James 2:14).

Step eleven encourages people in recovery to improve their conscious contact with God so that they may know his "will for us", essentially, so that they can do His bidding, which means live the life they were intended to live. The journey of individuation may involve a selfish retraction from society so that we can focus on our analysis. However, it is advised that once the process has been completed we should return to our communities and be effective in giving back from our abundant resources.

Step twelve

Having had a spiritual awakening as the result of these steps, we tried to carry this message to alcoholics, and to practice these principles in all our affairs

This step outlines in detail how a recovering alcoholic who is a member of A.A. can reinforce his sobriety by attempting to help another alcoholic achieve sobriety. One fellow alcoholic talking to another and sharing their experiences of sobriety, of living a sober life, is the essence of carrying the message that leads to a spiritual awakening and a complete and purposeful life.

Alex:

> When I arrived in A.A. over 17 years ago, completely and utterly beaten. I knew nothing about a spiritual awakening … I now appreciate that it is one of the most wonderful things that has ever happened to me. (*Share*, December 2013, p. 4)

John:

> While generally I may be a little mad, during one enlightening experience, I felt so calm and tranquil that being insane never occurred to me. It was at a time when I became aware of pollution and the mindless excessive use of the world's resources; I had been offered a second hand car by my employer, a charity who auctioned cars, at less than cost price. I was walking along thinking of buying it and suddenly became very aware of the multiple of cars passing me as though in a continuous loop, I became very conscious of my heart, as though I could see it, became enlarged as though my heart were a microcosm of the universe and in that moment I was the world; at that moment my heart spoke to me and said. "Not you too John." So I didn't buy the car! Normally I am very prudent

about such experiences, but I was confident enough to share this as a truly sane occurrence with a psychologist, but shocked when he diagnosed my experience as a hallucination. Since then I have been very sceptical of psychological diagnoses based on book learning! Even now, not so sure I had a spiritual experience as such, but am more aware of what's important in life and it sure isn't having the big car. No, now happy with the basics.

Yes I do try and spread the word to others about my good fortune of joining A.A., it's just like winning the lottery! With all the money and risky experiences I have been through with alcohol I realise that I have paid my entry dues to the club of A.A. And it sure is an expensive club to join. I do encourage others to join A.A., just as Bill Wilson did with Dr. Bob, simply one alcoholic talking to another helps reinforce my own sobriety. (Personal interview, 15 August 2013)

Explanation

When a person in A.A. undergoes their transformation or spiritual awakening, people, particularly family, friends and colleagues may notice and sometimes do comment on the healthy changes in the person, though they may not be able to say exactly what these changes are or how they came about. They may simply say there is a certain something different or as Dr. Silkworth said to Bill Wilson after he had his spiritual experience in Towns Hospital, "Something has happened to you I don't understand. But you had better hang on to it. Anything is better than the way you were" (Anon, 1991a, p. 14).

In relation to the second part of this step "to carry this message to alcoholics", the Big Book advises that, "Practical experience shows that nothing will so much insure immunity from drinking as intensive work with other alcoholics" (Anon, 1991a, p. 89). Indeed helping other alcoholics is fundamental to remaining sober. This working with a fellow alcoholic is the essence of the programme. After sobering up, Bill Wilson began a crusade of attempting to help other still suffering alcoholics. It dawned on Bill that the secret to his own sobriety was that he needed to talk to other alcoholics in order to remain sober. While he admitted he was not having much success with other alcoholics, he was aware that at least he himself was remaining sober as a result of this work.

Jungian perspective

So now that the twelve steps have been completed is there still a need to attend A.A. meetings? Yes, once fledgling sobriety is gained in A.A. it appears that a lifelong commitment of attendance at A.A. meetings is needed if sobriety is to be maintained. Jung explains, as though writing to remind A.A. members to "keep coming back" he states that "as soon as you are removed from the crowd, you are a different person again and unable to reproduce the state of mind" (CW 9i, para. 226). This means that the A.A. person in recovery needs to keep continually plugged into the meetings in order to retain their sobriety. This reminder to come back is again reinforced and further explained by Jung when he makes the observation that for any transformative change (drunkenness to sobriety) to be maintained, "You must have continual recourse to mass intoxication in order to consolidate the experience and your belief in it" (CW 9i, para. 226).

William James (1982) in his book recounts the stories of several people who recovered from alcohol and drug addiction including nicotine. The need for a connection with a Higher Power is illustrated by his account of one woman who was addicted to drugs,

> I had taken all the narcotics, stopped all work, been fed up, and in fact knew all the doctors within reach. But I never recovered permanently till this New Thought took possession of me. I think the one thing which impressed me most was learning the fact that we must be in absolutely constant relation or mental touch ... with that essence of life which permeates all and which we call God. (James, 1982, pp. 102–103)

This effectively is a forerunner to Jung's advice to Rowland Hazard and related in his letter to Bill Wilson when he wrote "spiritus contra spiritum" (see Appendix One).

James (1982) also wrote about Mr. Samuel. H. Hadley, an alcoholic based in New York's nineteenth-century skid-row Bowery, whose story of suicidal ideation is similar to that of many alcoholics who reach "rock bottom". After recovering he "became an active and useful rescuer of drunkards in New York" (James, 1982, p. 201) and his story is similar to Bill's story. As will be shown Hadley's example highlights the need for the recovering alcoholic to "pass it on" by working with active alcoholics and "newcomers" to A.A. in order to remain sober. The expression in A.A. is, "you have to give it away to keep it".

The following chapter will compare working the twelve steps and Jungian analysis.

Comparing the process of A.A. and Jungian analysis

Each of the twelve steps of the Alcoholics Anonymous programme plays a part in bringing the person dependent on alcohol from their "rock bottom" to a meeting with their spirit that is their true Self. In terms of the twelve steps this is called having a spiritual awakening.

Though the Jungian language is more sophisticated, the effects of "individuation" and a "spiritual awakening" are similar. Becoming individuated entails an increased dialogue between the conscious and the unconscious. In A.A. terminology the result of a spiritual awakening will be greater "God-consciousness". In simpler terms both roads may lead to a person developing their true potential and enjoying a greater appreciation of their place in this "wondrous Universe" (Sacks, 1985, pp. 26–30).

For the new analysand and the newcomer to A.A., concepts such as individuation and spiritual awakening are difficult to grasp. Alcoholics Anonymous attracts newcomers who simply want to stop drinking, if immediately offered a spiritual awakening there might be few takers. Similarly, people enter analysis initially to deal with a psychological difficulty; they are rarely looking for "individuation". Jungian analysis and A.A. do actually provide what they offer, but arguably the offer is a "loss leader"; namely, A.A. offers sobriety while Jungian analysis offers the prospect of peace of mind. However, in order to keep the sobriety and peace of mind, both acknowledge that a difficult journey has to be travelled, in particular relating to the submission of the ego.

While the Jungian individuation journey and the programme of A.A. have many similarities, so also do most of the great religions, including Christianity, Judaism, Islam, Hinduism, and the Eastern religions and philosophies such as Buddhism, the Kabbalah, and Freemasonry. These belief systems include much of the wisdom that is contained in the programme of Alcoholics Anonymous. For example, Freemasonry describes the human condition very succinctly:

> You are a threefold being. You have an outside personality, which functions in the world .... You also have an inside personality: a large psychological field called the mind. Your mind actuates the outside self (personality) ... But there is a third actor, beyond your outward person. A factor which joins you to the source of all beings. (Lomas, 2010, p. 88)

This "third actor" is our Spirit, our true Self, our Centre, our Soul. An explanation of this threefold being may be explained as follows: Firstly, that the "inside personality" is the ego, which functions in the outside world by using a persona (a personality). Secondly, that the "large psychological field called the mind" is our sense of being, who we are, what we call the small "self", which is primarily a combination of consciousness, ego and persona. Thirdly, and above all, but nonetheless hidden is "the third actor" which is our spirit or our true Self, indeed what we sometimes call our Soul.

The downfall of the person with an alcohol problem can be analysed from a Jungian perspective as follows: Normally, during the first half of life the ego, along with its ally the persona, facilitates the physical survival and development of the person by activities such as an apprenticeship, studying, finding a career, a mate, and a home. The persona can be used as a mask people wear to hide their true Self.

The persona is in the service of and under the control of the ego. In the form of teacher, tailor, soldier, sailor, the persona presents a civilised face to the world that allows the ego to negotiate its way through life. The ego may feel it is so successful that it does not want to let go of the reins of its power and ignores the pressing need to become in touch with the true Self. The ego thus forgets its purpose of being a vehicle that is supposed to facilitate the emergence of the true Self. It's as though the ego is the Ambassador for the King (the Self), but the ego as Ambassador decides that it is in fact the King and attempts to ignore the real King: the ego becomes a usurper of the function of the true Self.

According to Stephanie Covington, "The self that represents your outer identity is really only part of you. Your deep, inner Self is the self that is greater than who you seem to be on the surface" (Covington, 1994, p. 34).

The twelve steps of A.A. are not only about abstinence, but also involve a process of steps that facilitates the spiritual search that will lead a person back to a sense of wholeness and their true Self. The twelve steps of A.A. can be divided into four main stages: (1) Process of recovery begins with reaching a "rock bottom" and results in (2) a willingness to accept that there is a spiritual Higher Power. This leads to (3) confession; repentance; service in A.A.; and, through prayer and meditation, (4) attaining a spiritual awakening through conscious contact with God and then carrying the message of recovery to other alcoholics.

In the Jungian analytical analysis the stages are similar, but not necessarily in the same order. Entering analysis is usually accompanied by a deflation of the ego and may begin with a "confession" relating to past life. Secondly, elucidating the unconscious involves the analysand becoming aware of and accepting the existence of their more powerful unconscious. This may be the beginning of "a marked change in attitude, involving the individual in the sacrifice of (their) conscious intellect" (Samuels, 1986, p. 18).

The third stage is educational and usually begins with a confrontation with the shadow side of the ego—what in A.A. terminology are called defects of character. This may involve introjecting normally projected material so the analysand may increase their awareness of the "blind" side of their personality. This awareness will result in a person being more in control and less likely to be in the grip of unconscious complexes that usually focus on such sensitive areas as mothers, fathers, lovers, food, sex and money.

Additionally, the male may be more open to his feeling function which may manifest in the idealisation of a younger female figure—the stereotype of the old conformist professor suddenly running off with the young barmaid.

The female may become more aware of her animus (the male side of her personality) and become more assertive and develop a more independent personality, as opposed to being "the mother, daughter or wife of, etc".

The above stages may result in "the transformation process that loosens the attachment to the unconscious" (CW 9i, para 530). This is brought about by accepting, integrating, and assimilating opposite parts of the personality and making the unconscious more conscious. This may result in the person realising their full psychological potential, freeing them to become the person they were born to be. Overall, it may simply mean becoming more aware of the Soul or in A.A. terms, having a spiritual awakening.

The process of recovery from alcoholism is about deflation of the ego; a process whereby the ego has to submit to the service of the true Self. According to an expert on A.A., the solution to the divided self problem is a "crucifixion of the big 'I'. Surrender of self. A turning point involving self-surrender by the ego" (Dick, 1997, p. 140). Bill Wilson, writing in the "Big Book" (1991a), described the process of this submission of the ego to the true Self as acknowledging that "in this drama of life, God was going to be our Director. He is the Principal; we are his agents" (Ibid., p. 62). Similarly, David Schoen writes, "In religious terms, submission is often referred to as submitting to the will of God or the dictates of the Holy Spirit, or becoming one with the Buddha within" (Schoen, 2009 p. 17). Jung sees the ego as needing to eventually understand that it "will no longer be able to claim the central place but must presumably be satisfied with the position of a satellite, or at least of a planet revolving round the sun" (CW 12, para. 175).

This metaphor for the struggle between the ego and the unconscious involves a psychological wounding for the ego. Bill Wilson, writing "anonymously" in the book *Twelve Steps and Twelve Traditions* about the process of recovery from alcoholism, states, "Our eyes begin to open to the immense values which have come straight out of painful ego-puncturing" and that "in every case pain had been the price of admission into a new life" (Anon, 2002, p. 76).

The individuation process also involves an encounter between the ego and the Self. Jung compared the encounter between the ego and the Self to that of iron being forged between the "hammer and anvil" (CW 9i, para. 522). Similarly, for the alcoholic in recovery, there are many confrontations between the ego and the true Self. It usually begins with the first step when the ego admits powerlessness over alcohol. Then through working the twelve steps of A.A. the shadow part of the ego is confronted, acknowledged and assimilated by the ego, resulting in a "spiritual awakening". The "Big Book" of Alcoholics Anonymous (1991a) states that by actually working the twelve steps of Alcoholics Anonymous, "we have entered the world of the spirit" (p. 84).

The end result of a successful confrontation between ego and the true Self may result in a person becoming more whole. This necessitates reconciling all the various aspects of their personality, especially the ego with their true Self, and achieving a conscious insight into the energies of their unconscious.

The individuation process is similar to the journey of recovery entailed in the twelve steps, in that it is never fully accomplished. There is no such thing as "the individuated person," nor similarly is there "the recovered alcoholic". The process is in the journey and in both therapy and working the twelve steps it is the encounters on the way, whether with the unconscious or with people, that help create the end result. As with recovery from alcoholism the aim of the individuation process is always to seek progress, never expecting perfection.

CHAPTER SIX

Spiritual awakenings and cultism

Understanding spiritual experiences and spiritual awakenings

Twelve Steps and Twelve Traditions describes a spiritual wakening as:

> When a man or a woman has a spiritual awakening, the most important meaning of it is that he has now become able to do, feel and believe that which he could not do before on his unaided strength and resources alone. He has been granted a gift which amounts to a new state of consciousness and being .... He finds himself in possession of a degree of honesty, tolerance, unselfishness, peace of mind, and love of which he had thought himself quite incapable. (Anon, 2002, p. 110)

Most of the spiritual experiences that A.A. members have are "of an educational variety", in that they occur over an extended period of time. Some spiritual experiences can be short fleeting moments, as for example when Bill Wilson as a soldier visited Winchester Cathedral: "For a brief moment, I had needed and wanted God. There had been a humble willingness to have Him with me—and he came" (Anon, 1991a, p. 12).

Then there are the more dramatic spiritual experiences such as the type Bill Wilson had in Towns Hospital: "There was a sense of victory, followed by such a peace and serenity as I had never known" (Anon, 1991a, p. 14). While Bill did have a spectacular spiritual experience, he always said the end result was the same whether it was sudden spiritual experience or a gradual spiritual awakening—it led to the "personality change sufficient to bring about recovery from alcoholism" (Anon, 1991a, p. 569). Bill Wilson believed that all people who actually practice the twelve steps of A.A. eventually obtain a spiritual awakening (A.A. FAQ. (n.d.)).

As noted, Ebby Thacher while visiting Bill Wilson in Towns Hospital gave him a copy of William James's book, *The Varieties of Religious Experience*. Bill read and re-read this book and felt strengthened by the stories of spiritual experiences contained in the book (Anon, 2005, pp. 63–64).

William James (1982) understood that these spiritual experiences emanate from a source that cannot be conventionally categorised. He gave several examples of people in addiction having spiritual experiences. In particular, he quoted Mr. Samuel Hopkins Hadley's spiritual experience:

> One Tuesday evening I sat in a saloon in Harlem, a homeless, friendless, dying drunkard. I had pawned or sold everything that would bring a drink. I could not sleep unless I was dead drunk. I had not eaten for days, and for four nights preceding I had suffered with delirium tremens, or the horrors, from midnight till morning. I had often said, I will never be a tramp. I will never be cornered, for when that times comes, if ever it comes, I will find a home in the bottom of the river. But the Lord so ordered it that when the time did come I was not able to walk one quarter of the way to the river. As I sat there thinking, I seemed to feel some great and mighty presence. I did not know then what it was. I did learn afterwards that it was Jesus, the sinner's friend. I walked up to the bar and pounded it with my fist till I made the glasses rattle. Those who stood by drinking looked on with scornful curiosity. I said I would never take another drink, if I died on the street, and really I felt as though that would happen before morning. Something said, "If you want to keep this promise, go and have yourself locked up." I went to the nearest station-house and had myself locked up. In the prison cell ... that dear Spirit that came to me in the saloon

was present, and said "Pray." I did pray, and though I did not feel any great help, I kept on praying. (James, 1982, pp. 201–202)

When Hadley left the police station he went to stay with his brother:

> While lying in bed, the admonishing Spirit never left me, and when I arose the following Sabbath morning I felt that day would decide my fate … Oh, what a conflict was going on for my poor soul! A blessed whisper said, "Come"; the devil said, "Be careful." I halted but a moment, and then said, with a breaking heart, I said, "Dear Jesus, can you help me?" Never with mortal tongue can I describe that moment. Although up to that moment my soul had been filled with indescribable gloom, I felt the glorious brightness of the noon day sun shine into my heart. I felt I was a free man …. From that moment till now I have never wanted a drink of whiskey, and I have never seen money enough to make me take one. I promised God that night that I would work for him all my life. He has done his part, and I have been trying to do mine. (James, 1982, pp. 202–203)

Hadley began doing his "part", and this involved him becoming superintendent of a rescue mission for "skid-row" alcoholics in New York. His son, Henry also a recovering alcoholic, was in charge of the new Calvary Mission in New York from 1926 to 1933. Coincidently, it was in this Mission in December 1934 that Bill Wilson attended an Oxford Group meeting with Ebby Thacher and first tasted sobriety. Sam Shoemaker, rector of Calvary Episcopal Church in New York City, wrote that "I believe S. H. Hadley's conversion was extremely important—perhaps miraculous—as it relates to the events leading to the formation of Alcoholics Anonymous" (www.recoveryspeakers).

Wilson's and Hadley's spiritual experiences are similar to stories that some A.A. members recount about their Pauline road to Damascus moments of conversion. For example Mike a recovering alcoholic recalls:

> On my knees in that cell I cried out to my God: "Jesus help me remove the need to take any alcohol again." Nothing happened right away but I stayed on my knees listening in the quiet and I felt a movement in my midriff which moved up over my chest and

then over my head. I was shot into another dimension like our co founder Bill W. I then knew I was not having another drink for the rest of my life. (*Share*, February 2013, p. 5)

In Jungian terminology these Pauline conversions have a divine numinous quality about them. This means they are of "a dynamic agency or effect not caused by an arbitrary act of will. On the contrary, it seizes and controls the human subject, who is always rather its victim than its creator" (cited in Samuels, Shorter & Plant, 1986, p. 100).

These spiritual experiences also occur to members who have been sober for many years. One member who had seventeen years of sobriety wrote to Bill about his experience:

> I was alone in the hospital room at the time and am not sure whether I called out mentally or vocally. But at the instant of calling upon God I was taken out of my body ....
>
> What followed is important, though it will be very difficult to describe. For much of it there are no words. I will do the best I can.
>
> I appeared to be suspended in warmth, love, and an indescribable soft radiance which was not bright light and not darkness. Far away on all sides were millions of dots of clear light which were not stars, but each one a complete universe composed of millions of galaxies. This I knew. No one told me but the knowledge was given me, without words ....
>
> It was revealed to me that there is neither Matter nor Spirit, but only the will and the mind of God, that there is no substance but the substance of God in all things in all infinity.
>
> Questions arose in my mind and answers were supplied, mostly not in words. I thought, "Why am I held here in God's presence? Why do I not blow away through infinity like a blown leaf?"
>
> The answer came this time in words within me and I quote them exactly, for I feel that they apply to AAs most particularly (and were meant so to apply) as well as to all living things. "By the prayers ye have prayed, each for the other, are ye held up and supported one and all. By the deeds of love and mercy ye have done, each for the other, are ye held up and supported one and all ...."
> (*Grapevine*, December 1958: aagrapevine.org/node/24075, Beyond the fourth dimension).

On 28 July 1958 Bill Wilson replied:

> Your letter has been read and re-read and I've had copies struck off
> and shown it to many people. Beyond any question, it is a classical
> spiritual experience, and an illumination of the highest order. You
> certainly need to do no additional reading on the subject, as your
> experience takes in nearly every element reported in many cases on
> record, in volumes such as William James's Varieties of Religious
> Experiences (or Consciousness by Richard Buck). The letter you
> write is a tremendously moving and convincing document. The
> truth of what happened to you stands out in every line. I can say
> this with conviction and feeling because, as you know, I had one of
> these sudden experiences too. In principle, mine was identical. But
> I think that in detail and in brilliance yours is the finest I know, in
> AA or out. It is a great gift and I know that you will so treasure it
> always …. (AAA, 1958, Box 31, R14)

(For the full correspondence see Appendix Five.)

Are A.A. and Jungianism cults?

While it is outside the domain of this book, the question of whether
Jungianism and A.A. are cults should still be addressed, albeit briefly,
because both organisations have been subject to this criticism. This
chapter will consider the general and relevant characteristics of a cult
that may be applicable to Jungianism and A.A. In doing so, it will look
at some of the criticisms against A.A. and Jungianism, agree with some,
and offer a general defence to other points.

Firstly, according to Lalich and Langone (2006), the characteristics
of a cult include (A) an unquestioning loyalty and adherence to the
decisions of the leaders. (B) Cults may use "brainwashing techniques".
(C) They may engage in prostelysing, though "others" are often seen
as outsiders. (D) Dependence upon the group is encouraged so that
leaving it becomes difficult. (E) Members may see the leader as a
"messiah" on a special mission to save humanity. (F) Links with families may be discouraged. (G) There is a preoccupation with money and
group members may contribute large amounts of personal income or
time to the group.

Cults tend to attract vulnerable people who want to surrender
their own thinking process to a parental-type person or organisation.

Sometimes people in need are drawn to more powerful figures and actually like to create their own cult-type figures. It is probable that such people exist in A.A. and they no doubt become dependent and open to exploitation by sponsors and experienced members of A.A. Members who befriend and have sexual relationships with new members are known as "thirteen steppers".

Bill Wilson had a long-term mistress, Helen Wynn, a former actress and editor of the A.A. magazine *Grapevine* (Cheever, 2004, pp. 229–230). He is rumoured to have had relations with younger female members of A.A. and these unsubstantiated rumours are worthy of further enquiry, if only to stop them proliferating.

In relation to the first point above of unquestioning loyalty to a leader, Bill Wilson discouraged the cult of personality. He refused an offer from Yale University of an honorary degree of Doctor of Law and also refused to have his photo on the front of *Time* magazine, even with his back to the camera (Cheever, 2004, p. 229).

In terms of a cult, brainwashing means being mentally overpowered by outside influences that are against a person's own best interests and there is usually an element of exploitation involved. The submission to a Higher Power in A.A. and recitation of the slogans does have an element of brainwashing and there is a self-deprecating joke in A.A., that alcoholics do "need their brains washed". However, membership is voluntary and A.A. does not engage in prostelysing, indeed it states in its preamble that it is a programme of attraction rather than promotion.

Another distinguishing factor about cults is that there is a fear of leaving them, either through a threat or a dread of being isolated. It could be said that if a person leaves A.A., they will experience some separation anxiety because they are no longer part of the fellowship of people who are working the twelve-step programme. Will former A.A. members be shunned? Members of A.A. may be wary of former members who relapse and claim to be able to drink normally. They may fear that they will ask themselves, "Maybe I can do the same and control my drinking?" Most members of A.A. want to stick with the winners and will consider an alcoholic who is drinking to be in a sick state and may not wish to hear their "good news". Still, the beginning of most meetings includes a declaration welcoming back any members who have returned from a "slip". In practice, there is a prodigal welcoming back for members who relapse and then return to A.A. The attitude in A.A. is that alcoholics who have relapsed and returned to A.A. with their horror stories have done the research for members who remain sober.

Another mark of cults is that they tend to split people off from their relatives. Again one could say that A.A. takes up a person's time, usually in the evenings and thus they are separated from their families. In practice the time they do spend with their families is much valued and usually happier than when they were drinking.

Sometimes relatives arrange to hijack a person who has joined a cult? So far I have not heard of anyone being kidnapped and brought to an isolated place to be deprogrammed from A.A. The opposite is more usually the case, families may exclude the alcoholic from the family home until such time as they gain sobriety.

In relation to the general criticism of cults and their preoccupation with money, is A.A. money funnelled to a select few? There is an annual cap of approximately $3,000 on the amount a member may donate to A.A. Bill Wilson wrote the Big Book, and it is one of the bestselling books in the world, selling over thirty million copies. Wilson negotiated royalties from the sales of the Big Book and in his will bequeathed some of these royalties to his wife, Lois Wilson, and his mistress, Helen Wynn (Cheever, 2004, pp. 229–230). The Big Book is sold at a modest price of £8 sterling or $12 dollars, and its purchase is not obligatory.

Overall, as a side effect there are indeed cultish elements involved in membership of A.A. The major side effects are a psychological dependence on the organisation in order to remain sober and a social reliance on the friendships that develop amongst members. It might seem cultish that lifetime membership of A.A. is required to retain sobriety. However, it is not negative since it enhances the lives of recovering alcoholics. It could be considered that there is an addiction to A.A., yet recovering members, their partners, spouses, and employers endorse the conclusion that it is a positive addiction.

There are members who might see Bill Wilson and Dr. Bob as Messiahs. Some members of Alcoholics Anonymous believe that the writings of Bill Wilson were divinely inspired. Bill's writings can, by his own public admission, be directly attributed to the Oxford Group and "directly from Sam Shoemaker" (Anon, 2005, p. 39). Other influences include William James, the Bible and the Emanuel Movement.

The main proponents of A.A. being a cult are Charles Bufe (1998), who wrote *Alcoholics Anonymous: Cult or Cure?*, and Dr. Stanton Peele, who has written several books about addiction, including one co-authored with Charles Bufe and Archie Brodsky (2000), titled *Resisting 12-Step Coercion: How to Fight Forced Participation in AA, NA, or 12-step Treatment.* Their book makes a pertinent point about courts and rehabilitation centres pressuring people whom they consider to be abusing alcohol to attend A.A. According to this book, "Over 1,000,000 Americans are coerced into treatment annually, and probably nearly all are required to abstain from alcohol ..." (Peele, Bufe & Brodsky, 2000, p. 71). Perhaps "coerced" is too strong a word and might be replaced with the word "encouraged". Some rehab centres make it a condition that patients attend A.A. Indeed such coerced attendance is contrary to the policy of A.A. that prides itself on being "a program of attraction rather than promotion". Forced attendance at A.A. meetings in rehabilitation centres is a serious breach of the traditions of A.A. and needs to be addressed by the trustees of A.A. So Peele, Bufe and Brodsky are to be commended for highlighting these major breaches of A.A.'s own principles. In America, some secretaries of A.A. meetings will sign "chits" for people who have to prove to the courts that they have attended a meeting. More enlightened secretaries will sign the chits before the meeting thus giving unwilling participants the opportunity to prove they have attended and also to leave before the meeting starts. However, this signing of chits breaks the principle of anonymity.

Bufe's book, *Alcoholics Anonymous: Cult or cure?* lists several "secular" self-help groups for people with alcohol problems. His book gave Audrey Kishline, a problem drinker, and founder of "Moderation Management" (MM), three pages in which to extol the benefits of membership "not for the chronic and heavy drinkers" but to drinkers "who are concerned about their drinking" (Bufe, 1998, p. 171). Kishline claims that "the premises" of her programme are in part, "a development of ideas" by a group of world-renowned experts on alcohol addiction (Ibid.).

Arguably, "Moderation Management" is a variation on controlled drinking combined with educational material and group support with like-minded individuals. Based on over twenty years experience of therapeutic work with alcoholics who have tried to control their drinking, along with every permutation of every conceivable option, I consider "controlled drinking" for an alcoholic to be an oxymoron. The person who has a couple of drinks is in a relatively uninhibited state of mind compared to the person who first started drinking with the intention of only having a couple of drinks. To have to control your drinking is in itself an indication of a problem with an addictive drug. Controlled drinkers are literally playing with life and death. This was exampled by Audrey Kishline herself, who "continued drinking excessively", and in "March 2000, she drove her truck the wrong way down a highway and hit another vehicle head-on, killing its two passengers, a father and his 12 year-old daughter" (Moderation_Management, net).

Bufe writes from "insider" knowledge and bases his criticism, "from my attendance at scores of A.A. meetings in San Francisco in the mid and late 80s" (p. 86). His criticisms of A.A. and similarly those of Dr. Richard Noll, who criticises Carl Jung, deserve to be respected since they both have extensive knowledge of their subjects.

Is Jungianism a cult? Dr. Richard Noll is extremely critical of Jung in his writings, particularly, The *Jung Cult: Origins of a Charismatic Movement,* and also *The Aryan Christ: The Secret life of Carl Jung.* According to Bessinger (1997), the most relevant criticisms are that Jung developed his psychology as a religious cult with himself as an "Aryan Christ" saviour figure (p. 2). In relation to Jungianism being a cult, Noll also referred with some justification to Jung's "polygamy" (p. 159) and without justification to Jung's "God Complex" (p. 204). These criticisms have been tackled at length by Sonu Shamdasani (1998), Donivan Bessinger (1997), and John Haule (2000).

Shamdasani examined the claim by Noll that Jung effectively founded the cult of Jungianism in an inaugural address to the psychological club in Zurich in 1916. Shamdasani states that, "Were it not for this text and the claims made upon it, there is little in Noll's work that would merit further attention" (Shamdasani, 1998, p. 7).

A detailed defence of Noll's criticisms is outside the scope of this book. Instead, some personal remarks will be offered about my experience of Jungian training and analysis as "cultish".

To begin, Jung himself was reluctant to encourage a Jungian Institute to propagate his teachings. He said that he was glad that he was Jung and not a Jungian. Training as an analyst would appear to involve a cult-like commitment; a passionate personal, financial, and time commitment is required with little hope of recouping the expense. However one is free to leave anytime without any retribution. Candidates may initially believe they will become individuated, but this is a vague mercurial result which is never achieved. Are candidates brainwashed to believe Jungianism holds the answers to their own and the world's problems? I don't think so, but perhaps there is not enough emphasis on a critical evaluation of Jung's collected works. Sometimes the mere quoting of an apt phrase from Jung is made as a pronouncement and deemed to end a critical discussion. It is unlikely that Jung himself would have agreed to such adherence. In fairness the analytical training is open to and does take into account other psychological theories, including Cognitive Behavioural Therapy and even the organic psychiatric viewpoint.

The training may fulfill Lalich and Langone's point that links with families may be discouraged. Unfortunately, this is a reality in many professions and similarly analytical training requires enormous sacrifices by partners, spouses, and other members of the family. Yes, the Jungian training analysis is elitist, expensive and like many professions is arguably a pyramid system. However, there are generally positive results to the training in that a trained analyst usually becomes a useful contributing member of society.

Being in Jungian analysis usually involves one-to-three sessions a week. Analysts have a financial interest in encouraging analysands to attend for long periods of time, sometimes years. Certainly as part of the legitimate treatment, cult-like dependence may be deliberately fostered by the analyst through regression and transference. Arguably, the financial standing of the analysand may be a factor in this. However, the reality is that families generally encourage and support their members to be in analysis and while there are no records of kidnappings from analysis, there may be criticism when the person in analysis starts to become their own person and assert themselves. So the transformation that occurs in people in analysis and training analysis may upset relatives, but that is not a reason to designate it as a cult.

Again, it is outside the scope of this book to deal in detail with the many criticisms of A.A. and to a lesser extent Jungianism, though I hope that I have broadly answered those relating to cultism. I would suggest that overall such criticism can equally be applied to many clubs, fraternities, charitable organisations, political parties, businesses, and religions. No organisation is above censure, and criticism should be welcomed as it keeps the organisation alert to its potential to misuse its powers.

CONCLUSION

In a nutshell this book has attempted to show that the illness of alcoholism is a process involving a struggle between the ego and the true Self. In doing so it has tried to show the process involved, which includes ego deflation through reaching "rock bottom" and a resurrection of the true Self. This struggle may also occur in Jungian analysis. There is a similarity between the Jungian individuation process and working the twelve steps of Alcoholics Anonymous. The outcome of both processes are broadly similar in that it is the aim of both to facilitate the development of the whole person to their full potential through the realisation of the true Self.

Both processes, like many religions and philosophies, have broad generalities in common. In the first step of A.A. there is an admission of defeat; similarly walking across the threshold of the therapist's office is an admission that we cannot solve our problems alone, we need a guide. In both cases the journey is about the ego realising that the true Self is in control and that the ego's place is in the service of the Self.

The second step of A.A. advises that a belief in a greater power will restore sanity, and likewise in therapy we trust the analyst and hope to regain peace of mind.

In the third step of A.A. there is a turning over of the will and lives to a Higher Power. In therapy we don't go this far, but we do generally trust our therapist to put us in touch with our inner guide.

Steps four through to nine are all about preparing to make a full confession of moral deficiencies and making amends. Interestingly, Carl Jung has written that when making a confession it should first be written down; similarly, in A.A., it is suggested that when making a moral inventory in the fourth step that it be written down. Again Jung suggests that a confession must be to another person as in step five, "Admitted to God to ourselves and another human being". Most coincidently, Jung also makes the point that for a confession to be effective it needs to involve restitution as in step nine, "Made direct amends to such people wherever possible ..." Steps ten through twelve of A.A. are about building on and implementing the knowledge that was learned in the previous ten steps; the results may include the ego realising its function is to serve the Self and fellow beings and be of maximum service to God. Similarly in Jungian analysis, the "individuated" analysand will have found their true personality and "return" to benefit their community. Both "individuation" and completing the twelve steps usually involve a reconnection to society, a giving back. According to Jung, "The inner consolidation of the individual ... emphatically includes our fellow man" (CW 16, para. 444). Similarly the twelfth step encourages a person to engage with the world by actively carrying the message of recovery to fellow alcoholics.

The individuation process is similar to the journey of recovery entailed in the twelve steps, in that it is never fully accomplished. There is no such thing as "the individuated person," nor similarly is there "the recovered alcoholic". The process is in the journey and in both therapy and working the twelve steps it is the encounters on the way, whether with the unconscious or with people, that help create the end result. As with recovery from alcoholism the aim of the individuation process is always to seek progress, never expecting perfection.

In relation to the differences between the twelve-step journey and Jungian analysis, the obvious apparent difference is that A.A. is a group and Jungian analysis is individual and private. However, A.A., by encouraging sponsorship, also fulfils a similar function in relation to the privacy of a therapy session. Members are advised to be prudent in their public "confessions" in meetings and to reserve sensitive information for discussion with their sponsor. Additionally, members are also advised to seek outside help whenever they feel the need, since a sponsor is more like a close friend and is not qualified to deal with severe emotional issues which are outside their competence.

Another obvious feature is that A.A. is free, although a small donation to cover the cost of rent, literature, and refreshments is expected. The meetings of A.A. are similar to the first-century Gnostic Christian gatherings. The main difference between the Gnostics and orthodox Christians was that Gnostics believed in direct contact with God without any need for the mediation of priests or other religious officials. In contrast, some early Christians such as Bishop Irenaeus believed this notion was a heresy and a threat to the hierarchy of the church and insisted that it was necessary to go through a priest or deacon in order to communicate with God ("Irenaeus", 2014). This controversy gives a glimpse of the territoriality of religions. Arguably, the main difference between religion and spirituality is that in religion there are intermediaries between the person and God, whereas spiritual practice normally involves direct access. There appears to be an archetypal need or hunger for spiritual sustenance. Possibly A.A. and Jungian analysis have both helped people to reconnect with their individual spirituality and are unlike conventional religions with their emphasis on heaven and hell, and hierarchy of priests, bishops, rabbis and imams.

Who were the founders of A.A.? Bill Wilson was deliberately self-effacing on this issue; however, there is no doubt that he was the driving force and the principal founding father of A.A. Bill Wilson selflessly shared that honour with Dr. Bob Smith, his fellow co-founder. However, there were other early supporters who deserve similar recognition, not least the co-founder's respective wives: Lois Wilson and Anne Smith. These were extraordinary women who both kept informative journals on the workings and progress of A.A. Others deserving mention as founders members are Ebby Thacher, who first introduced Bill to the Oxford Group and became his sponsor; Mrs Henrietta Seiberling, related to the proprietors of the Akron-based Goodyear Tyre Company, who introduced Bill to Dr. Bob; Dr. Silkworth from Towns Hospital in New York; Reverend Samuel Shoemaker of the Oxford Group and Sister Ignatia Gavin, originally from Ireland, who supported Dr. Bob in his work in St. Thomas's Hospital in Akron. Underpinning spiritual supports are principally the Bible, the Oxford Group, the Emmanuel movement, and influential spiritual teachers such as Emmet Fox,

William James, and Carl Jung. Undoubtedly there are others (Cheever, 2012, Who really founded A.A.? thefix).

At first sight, it might appear that Bill Wilson's compliments to Jung were fawning. For example, he credited that "a certain conversation you once had with one of your patients, a Mr. Rowland H., back in the early 1930s, did play a critical role in the founding of our Fellowship" and wrote to him, thanking him for his part:

> So to you, to Dr. Shoemaker of the Oxford Groups, to William James, and to my own physician, Dr. Silkworth, we of A.A. owe this tremendous benefaction. As you will now clearly see, this aston-ishing chain of events actually started long ago in your consulting room, and it was directly founded upon your own humility and deep perception. (Bill Wilson's letter to Jung, 23 January 1961, see Appendix One)

Perhaps most strongly indicative of this praise was this sentence, "Please be certain that your place in the affection, and in the history of the Fellowship, is like no other" (Ibid.). So was Jung worthy of this praise?

Wilson had written to Jung that what "especially endeared yourself to us" was the fact that Jung understood the spiritual aspect of humans; that "man is something more than intellect, emotion, and two dollars worth of chemicals" (Ibid.). This in reality was a very brave stance for a "scientific" psychiatrist to take in the mid-twenties. No doubt it was reassuring for Bill to have one of the leading psychiatrists in the world endorse the view that alcoholism is a spiritual illness. So Wilson's praise was fitting. While the letter from Carl Jung gave A.A. increased credibility, Bill did seem to have a skill at bringing doctors on board, including Dr. Bob. Interestingly, his mother who abandoned him when he was ten years of age, went on to study to be an osteopathic physi-cian! (Kurtz, 1991, p. 10).

One of the many joys of researching this book was finding that the connection between Bill Wilson and Jung stretched back to the mid-forties. This was made possible through the travels and letters of Margarita Luttichau, a student of Jung's, whom both men mentored. They effectively communicated through the letters of Margarita. She introduced Wilson to Jung's philosophy on the spirituality of man, and in turn brought Wilson's ideas on the successful use of groups to Jung. Her letters to Bill Wilson shed new light on Jung's openness about applying therapeutic techniques with groups. In 1947, Jung gave Margarita "extraordinarily complete instructions" on how a group might be managed. Possibly for some Jungian adherents, Jung's apparent openness to groups is tantamount to an enantiodromia (a reversal or change of mind that brings psychic balance). However his willingness to change his ideas does show how flexible he could be. He devoted substantial attention to Margarita's accounts about the fledgling organisation of A.A. without then knowing it was destined to be a worldwide success.

There were other synchronistic finds, notably the clear line of descent between William James, Jung, Samuel Hadley, and Bill Wilson and their common acceptance of spirituality as a solution for alcoholism. James (1982) wrote "the only radical remedy I know for dipsomania is religio-mania, is a saying I have heard quoted from some medical men" (p. 268, fn 1). Jung is reputed to have based his phrase "spiritus contra spiritum" on this saying from William James. While it should be acknowledged that "some medical men" in the nineteenth century knew of the simple remedy for helping alcoholics, this wisdom was known as far back as the second century and expounded by the Roman Emperor, Marcus Aurelius to his soldiers "espiritum vinci espiritus" (Le Houx, 2013, p. 274). This translates as "holy spirit overcomes alcoholism" (Ibid.).

Alcoholics Anonymous, perhaps unwittingly, plays down the ultimate function of reconciling the person with themselves, effectively through a process similar to the Jungian individuation process. Indeed, A.A. tends not to emphasise its spiritual aim. Might the spiritual side of A.A. be a threat to religious orders that provide basement space for meetings? It is possible to speculate as to how far the alchemists were conscious of the true nature of their art. Similarly, one wonders if A.A. members when entering A.A. and even after many years are fully conscious that the aim of the programme is not just about gaining sobriety, but achieving a spiritual awakening of an educational variety?

A.A. has spread and gained acceptance throughout the world. Even in one-time apartheid South Africa, the regime allowed various races to attend A.A. meetings together. Today there are over two million members of A.A. in 116,000 groups in 180 nations. Alcoholics Anonymous literature has been translated into languages as diverse as Afrikaans, Arabic, Hindi, Nepali, Persian, Swahili, and Vietnamese, among many others (A.A. around the World, 2010).

Similarly, Jungian societies proliferate throughout the world, though Jungianism is still largely disregarded by scientific academic psychology (Adams, 2004). Perhaps the "wounded healers" need to remain on the outside to better understand their clients.

Today we are fortunate in the West that we live in comparatively enlightened times where we can be relatively open about our individual spiritual exploration. This journey may necessitate being a member of a group such as A.A. or being in analysis. Today there are still remnants of shame about attending A.A. or being in therapy. This stigma may harbour an archetypal reminder from "the collective" that today's tolerance may be a fleeting moment in the history of a normally fearful human race that prefers the certainty of dogma to the potential heresy of the "other" undertaking their own "secretive" and mystifying individual spiritual journey.

It is an open secret that Bill Wilson wrote a second letter to Carl Jung asking for his comments on prescribing LSD for alcoholics to help them gain a transcendent experience. However, it would appear that the trustees of A.A. hope that this letter should not be publicised. Ironically, A.A. have a guiding principle that "it is your secrets that will keep you sick". It is surely time, after fifty years, that this letter should now be fully debated. Wilson was a gifted creative social entrepreneur; he had the energy and the mindset of a discoverer and would not easily be restricted by the conservative trustees of the programme he had founded. Bill was unselfishly trying to persuade still-suffering alcoholics that there was a Higher Power in the universe that they could contact via a psychedelic experience. His aspiration was not to be realised due to the trustees' objections. He later described these trustees as "High Church people (who) might see claims a little bit contrary to certain aspects of their own doctrines" (AAA, 1958, Box 31, R 14). In fairness it should be stated that the trustees followed the advice of the preamble of A.A., which includes the following; A.A., "does not wish to engage in any controversy; neither endorses nor opposes any causes" (A.A. Preamble, Copyright © The AA *Grapevine*, Inc. Reprinted with permission).

Hopefully the debate on prescribing LSD to alcoholics in denial may be reopened. In September 2014, The British Psychologist Society magazine was devoted to psychedelic drugs. One of the main contributors concluded:

> The failure of the scientific community, particularly neuroscientists,
> to protest the denial of research on hallucinogens is one of the most

disturbing failures of science leadership in the past century, and it must be rectified. (*The Psychologist*, September 2014, 27: 9)

As already mentioned Bill Wilson did warn about the dangers of LSD becoming widely available. One member of A.A. wrote to me of his experiences with LSD and his views are worth quoting in full.

> LSD won't solve the problem of A.A.'s inherent contradictions.
>
> Indeed the idea that an active (or recently active) alcoholic, who is probably in a paranoid condition, could benefit from LSD is not a particularly good one, at best it is a gamble with not very good odds. LSD is a consciousness expanding drug and that expansion of consciousness may well extend into repressed memories and impulses about which the individual on LSD may have little or no awareness. There is no way to measure or anticipate how much expanded consciousness an individual will experience or can tolerate. The consequences of drug-induced expanded consciousness may last a lifetime, rather than just a few hours. Many people who have experienced LSD say it has permanently altered their consciousness of reality and I myself concur with that observation.
>
> I don't regret my experiences with LSD, I still value the connection with what seemed to be the vast and astonishingly beautiful intelligence of nature. However, one experience was potentially life threatening when during intense hallucinations, it seemed a seriously good idea to amputate my limbs, (fortunately there was no chainsaw or butchers cleaver nearby!) Generally I enjoyed the experience of hallucinogenic drugs, probably because of my psyche's ability to repress the many traumas I had experienced in a disturbed and violent childhood. I don't care however, to speculate on what would have occurred had these traumas surfaced while I was on these drugs as I was sometimes quite violent on alcohol.
>
> For a number of years after I stopped drinking and taking drugs my painting often became hallucinogenic and I suffered from what I can only describe as a psychic fragility which was often quite frightening. Some drug-using friends later told me that they too had a similar sense of psychic vulnerability. (Personal communication, 18 January 2015.)

My own impression, from working with alcoholics, some of whom have said that they would rather die than attend A.A., is that it is regretful that experiments into medical use of LSD did not continue then. It is probable that the suppression of LSD research may have had more to do with the politics of the times and its association with the Anti-Vietnam War movement, than objective scientific opinion.

Finally, as a footnote, Bill was also interested in treating alcoholics with Niacin (Vitamin B3). This is helpful to early recovering alcoholics who are depressed due to a deficiency in B vitamins. Poignantly, Bill wrote that he thought he would be remembered more for his promotion of Vitamin B3 than for co-founding A.A. (Kurtz, 1991, p. 138).

Bill Wilson—Carl Jung letters

January 23, 1961 Professor, Dr. C. G. Jung Kusnacht-Zurich Seestrasse 228 Switzerland.

My dear Dr. Jung:
   This letter of great appreciation has been very long overdue.

May I first introduce myself as Bill W., a co-founder of the Society of Alcoholics Anonymous. Though you have surely heard of us, I doubt if you are aware that a certain conversation you once had with one of your patients, a Mr. Rowland H., back in the early 1930's, did play a critical role in the founding of our Fellowship.

   Though Roland H. has long since passed away, the recollection of his remarkable experience while under treatment by you has definitely become part of A.A. history. Our remembrance of Rowland H.'s statements about his experience with you is as follows:

   Having exhausted other means of recovery from his alcoholism, it was about 1931 that he became your patient. I believe he remained under your care for perhaps a year. His admiration for you was boundless, and he left you with a feeling of much confidence.

   To his great consternation, he soon relapsed into intoxication. Certain that you were his "court of last resort," he again returned to your care. Then followed the conversation between you that was to become the first link in the chain of events that led to the founding of Alcoholics Anonymous.

My recollection of his account of that conversation is this: First of all, you frankly told him of his hopelessness, so far as any further medical or psychiatric treatment might be concerned. This candid and humble statement of yours was beyond doubt the first foundation stone upon which our Society has since been built.

Coming from you, one he so trusted and admired, the impact upon him was immense.

When he then asked you if there was any other hope, you told him that there might be, provided he could become the subject of a spiritual or religious experience—in short, a genuine conversion. You pointed out how such an experience, if brought about, might remotivate him when nothing else could. But you did caution, though, that while such experiences had sometimes brought recovery to alcoholics, they were, nevertheless, comparatively rare. You recommended that he place himself in a religious atmosphere and hope for the best. This I believe was the substance of your advice.

Shortly thereafter, Mr. H. joined the Oxford Groups, an evangelical movement then at the height of its success in Europe, and one with which you are doubtless familiar. You will remember their large emphasis upon the principles of self-survey, confession, restitution, and the giving of oneself in service to others. They strongly stressed meditation and prayer. In these surroundings, Rowland H. did find a conversion experience that released him for the time being from his compulsion to drink.

Returning to New York, he became very active with the "O.G." here, then led by an Episcopal clergyman, Dr. Samuel Shoemaker. Dr. Shoemaker had been one of the founders of that movement, and his was a powerful personality that carried immense sincerity and conviction.

At this time (1932–34) the Oxford Groups had already sobered a number of alcoholics, and Rowland, feeling that he could especially identify with these sufferers, addressed himself to the help of still others. One of these chanced to be an old schoolmate of mine, named Edwin T. He had been threatened with commitment to an institution, but Mr. H. and another ex-alcoholic "O. G." member procured his parole, and helped to bring about his sobriety.

Meanwhile, I had run the course of alcoholism and was threatened with commitment myself. Fortunately I had fallen under the care of a physician—a Dr. William D. Silkworth—who was wonderfully capable of understanding alcoholics. But just as you had given up on Rowland, so had he given me up. It was his theory that alcoholism had two components—an obsession that compelled the sufferer to drink against his will and interest, and some sort of metabolism difficulty which he then called an allergy. The alcoholic's compulsion guaranteed that the alcoholic's drinking would go on, and the allergy made sure that the sufferer would finally deteriorate, go insane, or die. Though I had been one of the few he had thought it possible to help, he was finally obliged to tell me of my hopelessness; I, too, would have to be locked up. To me, this was a shattering blow. Just as Rowland had been made ready for his conversion experience by you, so had my wonderful friend, Dr. Silkworth, prepared me.

Hearing of my plight, my friend Edwin T. came to see me at my home where I was drinking. By then, it was November 1934. I had long marked my friend Edwin for a hopeless case. Yet here he was in a very evident state of "release" which could by no means be accounted for by his mere association for a very short time with the Oxford Groups. Yet this obvious state of release, as distinguished from the usual depression, was tremendously convincing. Because he was a kindred sufferer, he could unquestionably communicate with me at great depth. I knew at once I must find an experience like his, or die.

Again I returned to Dr. Silkworth's care where I could be once more sobered and so gain a clearer view of my friend's experience of release, and of Rowland H.'s approach to him.

Clear once more of alcohol, I found myself terribly depressed. This seemed to be caused by my inability to gain the slightest faith. Edwin T. again visited me and repeated the simple Oxford Groups formulas. Soon after he left me I became even more depressed. In utter despair I cried out, "If there be a God, will He show Himself." There immediately came to me an illumination of enormous impact and dimension, something which I have since tried to describe in the book *Alcoholics Anonymous*, and also in *A.A. Comes of Age*, basic texts which I am sending to you.

My release from the alcohol obsession was immediate. At once I knew I was a free man.

Shortly following my experience, my friend Edwin came to the hospital, bringing me a copy of William James's *Varieties of Religious Experience*. This book gave me the realization that most conversion experiences, whatever their variety, do have a common denominator of ego collapse at depth. The individual faces an impossible dilemma. In my case the dilemma had been created by my compulsive drinking, and the deep feeling of hopelessness had been vastly deepened by my doctor. It was deepened still more by my alcoholic friend when he acquainted me with your verdict of hopelessness respecting Rowland H.

In the wake of my spiritual experience there came a vision of a society of alcoholics, each identifying with, and transmitting his experience to the next—chain-style. If each sufferer were to carry the news of the scientific hopelessness of alcoholism to each new prospect, he might be able to lay every newcomer wide open to a transforming spiritual experience. This concept proved to be the foundation of such success as Alcoholics Anonymous has since achieved. This has made conversion experiences—nearly every variety reported by James—available on almost wholesale basis. Our sustained recoveries over the last quarter-century number about 300,000. In America and through the world there are today 8,000 A.A. groups.

So to you, to Dr. Shoemaker of the Oxford Groups, to William James, and to my own physician, Dr. Silkworth, we of A.A. owe this tremendous benefaction. As you will now clearly see, this astonishing chain of events actually started long ago in your consulting room, and it was directly founded upon your own humility and deep perception.

Very many thoughtful A.A.s are students of your writings. Because of your conviction that man is something more than intellect, emotion, and two dollars' worth of chemicals, you have especially endeared yourself to us.

How our Society grew, developed its traditions for unity, and structured its functioning, will be seen in the texts and pamphlet material that I am sending you.

You will also be interested to learn that, in addition to the "spiritual experience," many A.A.s report a great variety of psychic phenomena, the cumulative weight of which is very considerable. Other members have—following their recovery in A.A.—been much helped by your practitioners. A few have been intrigued by the "I Ching" and your remarkable introduction to that work.

Please be certain that your place in the affection, and in the history, of our Fellowship is like no other.

Gratefully yours, William G. W.

Kusnacht-Zurich Seestrasse 228 January 30, 1961.

Mr. William G. W. Alcoholics Anonymous Box 459 Grand Central Station New York 17, New York.

Dear Mr. Wilson.
Your letter has been very welcome indeed.

I had no news from Roland H. anymore and often wondered what has been his fate. Our conversation which he has adequately reported to you had an aspect of which he did not know. The reason that I could not tell him everything was that those days I had to be exceedingly careful of what I said. I had found out that I was misunderstood in every possible way. Thus I was very careful when I talked to Roland H. But what I really thought about, was the result of many experiences with men of his kind.

His craving for alcohol was the equivalent, on a low level, of the spiritual thirst of our being for wholeness, expressed in medieval language: the union with God.[1]

How could one formulate such an insight in a language that is not misunderstood in our days?

The only right and legitimate way to such an experience is, that it happens to you in reality and it can only happen to you when you walk on a path which leads you to higher understanding. You might be led to that goal by an act of grace or through a personal and honest contact with friends, or through a higher education of the mind beyond the confines of mere rationalism. I see from your letter that Roland H. has chosen the second way, which was, under the circumstances, obviously the best one.

I am strongly convinced that the evil principle prevailing in this world leads the unrecognized spiritual need into perdition, if it is not counteracted either by real religious insight or by the protective wall of human community. An ordinary man, not protected by an action from above and isolated in society, cannot resist the power of evil, which is called very aptly the Devil. But the use of such words arouses so many mistakes that one can only keep aloof from them as much as possible.

These are the reasons why I could not give a full and sufficient explanation to Roland H. but I am risking it with you because I conclude from your very decent and honest letter that you have acquired a point of view above the misleading platitudes one usually hears about alcoholism.

You see, "alcohol" in Latin is "spiritus" and you use the same word for the highest religious experience as well as for the most depraving poison. The helpful formula therefore is: *spiritus contra spiritum.*

Thanking you again for your kind letter

I remain

yours sincerely

C. G. Jung

Appendix One

1. *"As the hart panteth after the water brooks, so panteth my soul after thee, O God" (Psalm 42, 1)*

Twelve steps of A.A.

1. We admitted we were powerless over alcohol—that our lives had become unmanageable.
2. Came to believe that a Power greater than ourselves could restore us to sanity.
3. Made a decision to turn our will and our lives over to the care of God *as we understood Him.*
4. Made a searching and fearless moral inventory of ourselves.
5. Admitted to God, to ourselves, and to another human being the exact nature of our wrongs.
6. Were entirely ready to have God remove all these defects of character.
7. Humbly asked Him to remove our shortcomings.
8. Made a list of all persons we had harmed, and became willing to make amends to them all.
9. Made direct amends to such people wherever possible, except when to do so would injure them or others.
10. Continued to take personal inventory and when we were wrong promptly admitted it.

11. Sought through prayer and meditation to improve our conscious contact with God as we understood Him, praying only for knowledge of His will for us and the power to carry that out.
12. Having had a spiritual awakening as the result of these steps, we tried to carry this message to others, and to practice these principles in all our affairs.

Reprinted with Permission of A.A. World Services, Inc.

Twelve traditions

1. Our common welfare should come first; personal recovery depends on A.A. unity.
2. For our group purpose there is but one authority—a loving God as He may express Himself in our group conscience. Our leaders are but trusted servants; they do not govern.
3. The only requirement for A.A. membership is a desire to stop drinking.
4. Each group should be autonomous except in matters affecting other groups or A.A. as a whole.
5. Each group has but one primary purpose—to carry its message to the alcoholic who still suffers.
6. An A.A. group ought never endorse, finance, or lend the A.A. name to any related facility or outside enterprise, lest problems of money, property, and prestige divert us from our primary purpose.
7. Every group ought to be fully self-supporting, declining outside contributions.
8. Alcoholics Anonymous should remain forever nonprofessional, but our service centers may employ special workers.
9. A.A., as such ought never be organized; but we may create service boards or committees directly responsible to those they serve.

10. Alcoholics Anonymous has no opinion on outside issues; hence the A.A. name ought never be drawn into controversy.
11. Our public relations policy is based on attraction rather than promotion; we need always maintain personal anonymity at the level of press, radio, and films.
12. Anonymity is the spiritual foundation of all our Traditions, ever reminding us to place principles above personalities.

The twelve promises of Alcoholics Anonymous

1. If we are painstaking about this phase of our development, we will be amazed before we are half way through.
2. We are going to know a new freedom and a new happiness.
3. We will not regret the past nor wish to shut the door on it.
4. We will comprehend the word serenity and we will know peace.
5. No matter how far down the scale we have gone, we will see how our experience can benefit others.
6. That feeling of uselessness and self-pity will disappear.
7. We will lose interest in selfish things and gain interest in our fellows.
8. Self-seeking will slip away.
9. Our whole attitude and outlook upon life will change.
10. Fear of people and of economic insecurity will leave us.
11. We will intuitively know how to handle situations which used to baffle us.
12. We will suddenly realise that God is doing for us what we could not do for ourselves.

Are these extravagant promises? We think not. They are being fulfilled among us—sometimes quickly, sometimes slowly. They will always materialize if we work for them.

Reprinted from *Alcoholics Anonymous,* pp. 83–84, with permission of A.A. World Services, Inc.

Bill corresponds with an A.A. member about his spiritual experience

Bill Wilson received many letters from members describing spiritual awakenings that were similar to the one he experienced in Towns Hospital. He called it the fourth dimension. Writing to a member in April 1958, Bill explained what he meant by a "fourth dimension" spiritual experience: "I was catapulted to a spiritual experience that gave me the capability of feeling the presence for God, His love, His omnipotence. And most of all, his personal availability to me. Of course this is the ABC of the conversion experience—something as old as man himself. So maybe an awareness of God and some sense of relation to Him constitutes a fourth dimension. At least this was true for me, one who had no belief or such sensibility whatever."

Bill considered that the only difference between his own transforming experiences and that of members who work the programme is that his own experience "was lightning fast—I experienced in months what most AAs receive in years. That, in my view, is the only and not too important difference" (AAA, 1958 Box 31, R 14).

Bill received one particular letter from a member that he felt should be publicised. This letter gives a good overall representation of the type of spiritual experiences Bill was privy to. Because of its comprehensiveness as a good general representation of spiritual experience it is worth quoting in full. It is dated 16 June 1958 and reads:

DEAR BILL,

I am writing this in the form of a letter to you personally so that you may read and then make whatever disposition of it you may feel best— short of breaking my anonymity. I do not know if you, or AA, keep a file of records of such experiences. If so, I think that this should be included.

> This is the record of what I believe to have been a most profound and important spiritual experience, set down just as it took place.
>
> On Easter Sunday of this year I was taken from my home to the Victoria Hospital in Miami. I was suffering from a massive *lobal croupus* pneumonia of the right lung and was placed in an oxygen tent the same day. My physician was Dr. Samuel Page, Jr., of Miami. At that date I had been a practicing member of AA, sober, without ever having a slip, for almost exactly seventeen years.
>
> From Sunday through the following Thursday I remained under oxygen in an increasingly critical condition and almost continuously out of my head. Because of some element in my blood the "miracle drugs" administered to me had no effect and my condition grew steadily worse. By Thursday evening it was not certain that I would live through the night. My right lung was full of material so gummy that attempts to tap the lung had failed.
>
> During the night, in spite of delirium, I became increasingly aware of my condition … at first struggling desperately, then feeling weakness and despair until suddenly, at the depths, and Knowing myself to be at the point of death I remembered the most blessed Eleventh Step and called upon God to give me the strength to do His will, even at the extremity. I was alone in the hospital room at the time and am not sure whether I called out mentally or vocally.
>
> But at the instant of calling upon God I was taken out of my body. There was no feeling of transition. Only an instant cessation of pain and immediate feeling of the most wonderful peace, love, and understanding. My body was left behind, but with no more feeling of loss than a deep sea diver might feel at leaving his shell of leather and steel. The essence, the totality of me was intact and I knew that I could have another body if I wished.

I knew that I was no longer at or near our earth but whether I had been moved in space, in time or into another dimension entirely was neither apparent nor important. Nor do I know how long the experience lasted; to me it seemed a continual time but I believe that it may have been very short by earth time. It is not very important.

What followed is important, though it will be very difficult to describe. For much of it there are no words. I will do the best I can.

I appeared to be suspended in warmth, love, and an indescribable soft radiance which was not bright light and not darkness. Far away on all sides were millions of dots of clear light which were not stars, but each one a complete universe composed of millions of galaxies. This I knew. No one told me but the knowledge was given me, without words. Through these myriads of universes there ran tides of currents which moved them in an ordered manner, softly but with infinite power. Again I Knew. Each of these "tides" was a thought of God. I Sensed, I Knew, I Felt the thoughts of God move about me, in me, in all infinity.

It was revealed to me that there is neither Matter nor Spirit, but only the will and the mind of God, that there is no substance but the substance of God in all things in all infinity.

Questions arose in my mind and answers were supplied, mostly not in words. I thought, "Why am I held here in God's presence? Why do I not blow away through infinity like a blown leaf?"

The answer came this time in words within me and I quote them exactly, for I feel that they apply to AAs most particularly (and were meant so to apply) as well as to all living things. "By the prayers ye have prayed, each for the other, are ye held up and supported one and all. By the deeds of love and mercy ye have done, each for the other, are ye held up and supported one and all."

There were other questions, other knowledge imparted in answer. Many things that I cannot express.

There was love, understanding (He marketh the sparrow's fall), peace beyond any description. I saw neither visions nor angels. I felt myself to be WITHIN the being and presence of God and that his attention was directed to me. As each of us is an individual and yet a member of the BODY of humanity, so each is an individual and a member of the BODY of God.

There was no feeling of weight of sin or shame, no last judgment, only peace. I knew that I had taken our AA spiritual teachings and way of life in some way ACROSS the boundary, through the gateway from earthly life to life eternal. I knew immortality. I knew death was but an awakening. I knew that I was not dead, then, suddenly knew that if I did not return to my body I would have died. Again the 11th step, what is Thy will, O God? And the answer (perhaps the most astounding part of the whole experience). I was offered a choice. By an act of will I could remain with God. But for some reason (not clear) I felt that he wanted me to choose to return to this earth.

As soon as I accepted this idea I was back in my bed in the hospital, back in my body again, but rational, calm and assured of recovery. From that moment my body healed at a very rapid rate and far beyond expectation for a man of my age (46)-I have not discussed this with the doctor but with my wife and a few friends in AA.

I am perfectly convinced that all occurred just as I have set down. I do not know why God wanted me to live, but accept His will without question.

Now to set down some random recollections and deductions from this experience. During the whole time of the experience my personality was intact, my brain clear and calm. From the instant of consciously employing the 11th step there was no fear at all. I knew myself to be at the point of death, but faith triumphed.

THE PROGRAMME CAN BE CARRIED TO AND THROUGH THE DOORWAY OF ETERNITY and it will work for us. That is one of the most tremendous facts of the whole experience. The program is so keyed to our reason for being here in the first place that we Do take it with us.

We are here on earth to learn and to grow spiritually. The nature of God is true and perfect love. All living things are not only assured of immortality, but are now and forever in process of immortality.

The dividing line between "life" and "death" is apparent or illusory rather than existent. Prayers cross it in one direction, miracles and love return.

I have no idea why God wished me to live. Certainly it is not that I am "important or unusual" in any way. I know that since the experience many old angers and resentments, some of thirty years' standing, have vanished as if washed away, that I feel a continued and growing inner happiness ADDED to my being.

I would appreciate hearing from you after you read this. Edward

(Grateful acknowledgement to *Grapevine* for permission to quote the above correspondence published in their magazine under the title: *Beyond the 4th Dimension*, December 1958).

Bill Wilson's reply to the A.A. Member

On 28 July 1958 Bill replied: (AAA, 1958, Box 31, R 14).

Your letter has been read and re-read and I've had copies struck off and shown it to many people. Beyond any question, it is a classical spiritual experience, and an illumination of the highest order. You certainly need to do no additional reading on the subject, as your experience takes in nearly every element reported in many cases on record, in volumes such as William James's Varieties of Religious Experiences (or Consciousness by Richard Buck). The letter you write is a tremendously moving and convincing document. The truth of what happened to you stands out in every line. I can say this with conviction and feeling because, as you know, I had one of these sudden experiences too. In principle, mine was identical. But I think that in detail and in brilliance yours is the finest I know, in AA or out. It is a great gift and I know that you will so treasure it always.

Doubtless you have gone on wondering why this experience came to you. As time goes on, you may find out or you may not. It is my belief that what you and I have received so suddenly is actually received by every AA. In cases like ours, the ego seems to break down completely, if only momentarily, consequently there is an immense influx of grace, making for the sudden illumination. For the average AA the ego bends but does not fully break, so that grace leaks in more slowly.

I might add this: while these sudden experiences have tremendous advantages of assurance, they do have their liabilities. I'm sure you will not fall under the error that i did. In my own case, I thought I was rather specially "anointed" to save all the drunks in the world. It took me about a year of stark failure to accomplish anything, to convince me that I was only one of many; that I should be grateful for my gift but never conceited by it.

Your letter is in the hands of the Grapevine. Of course your anonymity will be preserved. Whether the Board will conclude to publish it—or all of it- I cannot say. Personally I believe they should and I think I ought to write a header for the document which will encourage other AA's to send in similar accounts. There are probably a great many such experiences of which we know nothing. The only objection to publication is that the High Church people might see claims a little bit contrary to certain aspects of their own doctrines. But I don't think there is enough difficulty of this sort to put the lid on this immensely inspiring account which you give.

I regret very much that I cannot go into an extensive discussion of this matter of spiritual experience because of the great pressure of affairs. Supposedly I retired from it in 1965, but have never been so busy. However, I'm not busy running AA, I'm only cleaning up some chores still undone, at the time AA came of age. Everyone who has read your letter sends their gratitude because the inspiration of your experience has come to them as well as to you. If you feel in a mood write more,

Devotedly Bill Wilson

The third page of Bill Wilson's second letter to Jung dated 20 March 1961 (Kindly forwarded by a confidential source)

Then, too, there is a development now going on in the area of spiritual or mystical experiences which were triggered by the use of LSD, a synthetic alkaloid having a chemical kinship with a rare Mexican mushroom and with the Peyote cactus button of America's western plains. As perhaps you know, many psychiatrists still cling to the conviction that these LSD experiences are always schizophrenia and rather dangerous. Yet hard evidence has been accumulating that this is seldom the case. Lysergic acid (LSD) is very truly harmless and quite non addictive. Some of my AA friends and I have taken the material frequently—and with much benefit. Once in the experience, there is a great broadening and deepening and heightening of consciousness, which bares little or no relation to hallucination. More reality is seen, and felt—not less. We have seen the whole range of valid spiritual experience precipitated in this manner. On my first trial several years ago, my original spontaneous spiritual experience of twenty-five years before was re-enacted in wonderful splendor and conviction.

Because of a close contact with two physicians, Drs. Abram Hoffer and Humphry Osmond of the University of Saskatchewan, Canada, I have access to case material covering thousands of administrations there and world-wide. These friends (each of them a psychiatrist and a bio-chemist) were no doubt the first physicians to see a spiritual significance in LSD. Their very large experience has made it impossible for them to deny the "objective reality" of most of these experiences they have seen, and indeed, have had themselves. My friends have many alcoholics in their charge at the Provincial Mental Hospital. As you well know, these would be extremely difficult cases, even after having excluded marked psychotics. AA gets about a 5% recovery rate in such cases. But if these alcoholics are first preconditioned by LSD and then placed in the surrounding AA groups, the result is startling. Over the past three years, 150 cases have been so treated by my Canadian friends. As of this writing, seventy-five are remaining perfectly sober in the outside world. This scarcely squares with the wide-spread view that LSC is dangerous and hallucinatory!

My friends believe that LSD temporarily triggers a change in blood chemistry that inhibits or reduces ego, thereby enabling more reality to be felt and seen. The amount of LSD needed is extremely small and the material seems to be eliminated from the body before the experience begins. Little effect is noted in the first hour—but the experience continues for many hours. It may be, chemically speaking, that the predisposing affect of LSD bears some relation to what may chemically occur in ascetic practices such as fasting, Yoga exercise and the like.

Of course these LSD manifestations are deeply shocking to many theologians, and even psychiatrists. Yet a total of 50,000 administrations in the US and Canada during the past seven or eight years has resulted in virtually no harm and certainly large benefits to many.

I've entered these observations for your interest and, if agreeable, for your comment. But please do be assured that it will be perfectly understood if your time, inclination or health should not permit you to reply.

Mainly I am writing in thanks for your recent message, and again to record the deep gratitude of our AA Fellowship for your signal contributions to its welfare over the years.

Most sincerely,
William G. Wilson Co-Founder, A.A.

NOTES

Introduction

1. The origin of the term "Big Book" came from the fact that the first printing of the first edition of the book was almost two inches thick. It was deliberately printed on very heavy paper. The reason for the thick paper was because they wanted to sell the book for $3.50 each so because it was such a big book people would feel they were getting their money's worth. Adjusted for inflation that would bring the price to approximately $50 or £35.

2. "Rock-bottom"—The *Oxford English Dictionary* gives the following definition of the term: "rock-bottom, bed-rock; also *fig.*, the fundamental or lowest possible level, nadir. [1856 'OLD COLONIST' *How to Farm & Settle in Austral.*] This lowest bottom, 'the rock' as it is emphatically termed, in reference to its character as a bar to further digging for gold."

Chapter One

1. Margarita Pennington Luttichau transcribed a summary of a talk by Victor White on the Sermon of the Mount that was published in the Jungian Club's Bulletin, 10 March 1948, pp. 6–8.

2. The Oxford Group was a Christian organisation founded by American Christian missionary Dr. Frank Buchman. He was an American Lutheran minister of Swiss descent who in 1908 had a conversion experience in a chapel in Keswick, England and as a result of that experience he would later found a movement called A First Century Christian Fellowship in 1921, which eventually became known as the Oxford Group by 1931.

3. Aniela Jaffe, a Jungian analyst and author, acted as a personal assistant to Jung in his final years She is credited with shadow writing most of Jung's "autobiography", *Memories, Dreams, Reflections* (1985).

4. This book had been given to Wilson by Margarita Luttichau many years previously in 1945 (AAA, Box 18, R8).

5. In 1943, Albert Hoffman, a Chemist in Basle while working with the compounds of LSD, accidentally absorbed a small quantity and discovered its powerful effects. Ian Baker (1968) quotes from Hoffmann's notebook "I had to leave my work at the laboratory and go home because I felt strangely restless and dizzy. Once there I lay down and sunk into a not unpleasant delirium which was marked by an extreme degree of fantasy. In a sort of trance with closed eyes (I found daylight unpleasantly glaring) fantastic visions of extraordinary vividness accompanied by a kaleidoscopic play of intense coloration continuously swirled around me. After two hours this condition subsided."

Chapter Two

1. Bill Wilson may have transcribed the inscription from the Tombstone as he only got a few words wrong. A.A. produce a leaflet explaining the connection between the Tombstone and A.A., and it is available in Winchester Cathedral.

2. The distinction between a spiritual awakening and spiritual experience "is that a Spiritual Experience is relatively sudden, lasting only minutes or perhaps a few hours while a Spiritual Awakening is a gradual transformation that can take days, weeks, and months or even longer; Prof. William James described a spiritual awakening as an experience of the educational variety. In his writings, Bill Wilson explained the difference, noting that among A.A. members who perform all the spiritual exercises described as 'the steps', experiences like his are far less common than spiritual awakenings. In any event, the result is the same; the individual has a personality change sufficient to recover from alcoholism" (A.A. FAQ, n.d.).

Chapter Three

1. The Zofingia Club was a discussion group to which C. G. Jung belonged as a medical student. He was elected Chairman in 1897 and gave five lectures.

Chapter Five

1. I am indebted to Dr. Finbar O' Mahony for this point.

REFERENCES

A.A. Around the World. (2010). 75 years of growth: The spread of A.A.'s message. Retrieved from www.aa.org/pages/en_US/aa-timeline last accesssed 20 March 2015.

A.A. FAQ. (n.d.). Spiritual awakening vs. spiritual experience. Retrieved from www.anonpress.org/faq/467?password=ChumpSuck5000! Last accessed 20 March 2015.

Abraham, L. (1998). *Dictionary of Alchemical Imagery*. Cambridge, UK: Cambridge University Press.

Adams, M. V. (2004). If the university won't have Jungians, then how might Jungians have the university? Retrieved from www.jungnewyork.com/univ_jung.shtml last accessed 6 March 2015.

Alexander, J. (1941). Alcoholics Anonymous: Freed slaves of drink, now they free others. *The Saturday Evening Post*, 59–65.

americancatholic.org/e-News/FriarJack/fj093009.asp last accessed 20 March 2015.

American Psychiatric Association. (2013). *Diagnostic and Statistical Manual of Mental Disorders* (5th ed.). Washington, DC: American Psychiatric Association.

Anonymous. (1963). The Bill Wilson—Carl Jung letters. *The Grapevine*, 14(1): 22–28.

Anonymous. (1979). *Lois Remembers: Memoirs of the Co-founder of Al-Anon and Wife of the Co-founder of Alcoholics Anonymous*. New York, NY: Al-Anon Family Group Headquarters, Inc.

Anonymous. (1991a). *Alcoholics Anonymous: The Story of How Many Thousands of Men and Women have Recovered from Alcoholism (the Big Book)* (3rd ed.). New York, NY: Alcoholics Anonymous World Services.

Anonymous. (1991b). *Pass It On: The Story of Bill Wilson and How the A.A. Message Reached the World*. New York, NY: World Services, Inc.

Anonymous. (2000). *Bill W.: My First 40 Years*. Center City, MN: Hazelden.

Anonymous. (2002). *Twelve Steps and Twelve Traditions*. New York, NY: World Services, Inc.

Anonymous. (2005). *Alcoholics Anonymous Comes of Age: A Brief History of A.A.* New York, NY: Alcoholics Anonymous World Services.

Anonymous. (2011). *The Book that Started It All: The Original Working Manuscript of Alcoholics Anonymous*. Center City, MN: Hazelden.

Aware. (n.d.). Information about our support groups. Retrieved from www.yourhealthinmind.org/cmsfiles/Leaflets/Aware-Support-Groups.pdf last accessed 6 March 2015.

Baker, I. F. (1968). *LSD 25 & Analytical Psychology* (Doctoral book). C. G. Jung Library, Kusnacht, Switzerland. (Reference No. KT 66 02) [I am indebted to Tess Castleman for this source].

Bauer, J. (1982). *Alcoholism and Women: The Background and the Psychology*. Toronto, CA: Inner City Books.

Beebe, J. (Ed.). (1983). Money, food, drink, and fashion and analytic training. Depth dimensions of physical existence. The proceedings of the Eighth International Congress For Analytical Psychology. Fellbach-Oeffingen (Verlag Adolf Bonz GmbH).

Bessinger, D. (1997). Cult and controversy: Richard Noll versus Carl G. Jung. http://home.earthlink.net/~dbscr/pler/Nollcult.htm last accessed 12 March 2015.

Bible (Gideons International).

Big Book. (n.d.). In: *Wikipedia the Free Encyclopedia*. Retrieved from http://en.wikipedia.org/wiki/The_Big_Book_ last accesssed 6 March 2015.

Blocker, J., Fahey, D., Tyrrell, I. (Eds.) (2003). *Alcohol and Temperance in Modern History: A Global Encylpopaedia*. Santa Barbara: ABC Clio.

Bluhm, A. (2006). Verification of C. G. Jung's analysis of Rowland Hazard and the history of Alcoholics Anonymous. *History of Psychology, 9*: 313–324.

Brewer, M. (1987). Pabola. *Collection, 12*: 4–5.

Bufe, C. (1998). *Alcoholics Anonymous: Cult or cure?* Tucson, AZ: Sharp Press.

Castleman, T. (2009). Sacred dream circles: A guide to facilitating Jungian dream groups. Einsiedeln, Switzerland: Daimon Verlag.

Cheever, S. (2004). *Bill Wilson: His Life and the Creation of Alcoholics Anonymous*. New York, NY: Simon & Schuster.

Cheever, S. (2012). Who really founded A.A.? *The fix: Addiction and recovery, straight up*. Retrieved from www.thefix.com/content/bill-w-dr-bob-real-founder-aa (last accessed 20 March 2015).

Colman, A. (1995). *Up from Scapegoating. Awakening Consciousness in Groups*. Wilmette, Illinois: Chiron Publications.

Confess. (2014). In: *Oxford Dictionaries*. Retrieved from www.oxforddiction aries.com/definition/english/confess last accessed 6 March 2015.

Covington, S. (1994). *A Woman's Way Through the Twelve Steps*. Minneapolis, MI: Hazelden.

Dick, B. (1997). *The Good Book and the Big Book: A.A.'s Roots in the Bible*. Kihei, HI: Paradise Research Publications, Inc.

Dick, B. (1998). The Oxford Group & Alcoholics Anonymous: A Design for Living that Works. Kihei, HI: Paradise Research Publications, Inc.

Doe, J. (1950). *The Golden Book of Action*. Minneapolis, MI: Hazelden.

Fellowship. (2014). In: *Collins English Dictionary*. Retrieved from www. collinsdictionary.com/dictionary/english/fellowship?showCookiePoli cy=true last accessed 6 March 2015.

Freud, S., & Jung, C. G. (1979). *The Freud/Jung letters [Abridged]*. W. McGuire (Ed.), R. F. C. Hull & R. Manheim (Trans.), Abridged by Alan McGlashan. Princeton, NJ: Princeton University Press.

Gately, I. (2008). *Drink: A Cultural History of Alcohol*. New York, NY: Gotham Books. goodreads.com—www.goodreads.com last accessed 20 March 2015.

Gorski, T. P. (1989). *Passages Through Recovery: An Action Plan for Preventing Relapse*. Center City, MN: Hazelden.

Grapevine Magazine, online: http://www.aagrapevine.org/ last accessed 6 March 2015.

Hannah, B. (1976). *Jung: His Life and Work*. New York, NY: G. P. Putnam and Sons.

Haule, J. (2000). Waiting For C. G.: A Review of the biographies. *Quadrant, XXX* (1), 71–87. Retrieved from www.jrhaule.net/waiting4CG.html last accessed 6 March 2015.

Hoffer, A., & Osmond, H. (1968). *New Hope for Alcoholics*. New York, NY: University Books.

Hopcke, R. H. (1989). *A Guided Tour of the Collected Works of C. G. Jung*. Boston, MA: Shambhala Publications, Inc.

Humble. (2014). In: *Collins English Dictionary*. Retrieved from www. collinsdictionary.com/dictionary/english/humble?showCookie Policy=true last accessed 6 March 2015.

Irenaeus. (n.d.). In: *Wikipedia the Free Encyclopedia*. Retrieved from http:// en.wikipedia.org/wiki/Irenaeus last accessed 6 March 2015.

Jaffe, A. (Ed.). (1970). *C. G. Jung Word and Image* (Bollingen Series XCV11). Princeton, NJ: Princeton University Press.

Jaffe, A. (Ed.). (1985). *Memories, Dreams, Reflections* by C. G. Jung. London, UK: Collins and Routledge and Keegan Paul.

James, W. (1982). *The Varieties of Religious Experience.* London, UK: Penguin.

Jung, C. G. (1945). *Modern Man in Search of a Soul.* London, UK: Kegan Paul, Trench, Truber & Co.

Jung, C. G. (1957). Psychiatric studies. H. Read (Ed.), *The Collected Works of C. G. Jung* (R. F. C. Hall, Trans.) (CW 1). Princeton, NJ: Princeton University Press.

Jung, C. G. (1969). Psychology and religion—west and east. H. Read (Ed.), *The Collected Works of C. G. Jung* (R. F. C. Hall, Trans.) (CW 11). Princeton, NJ: Princeton University Press.

Jung, C. G. (1972). Two Essays on analytical psychology. H. Read (Ed.), *The Collected Works of C. G. Jung* (R. F. C. Hall, Trans.) (CW 7). Princeton, NJ: Princeton University Press.

Jung, C. G. (1974). *The Undiscovered Self.* London: Routledge & Kegan Paul.

Jung, C. G. (1976). *Selected Letters of C. G. Jung, 1951–1961.* Vol. 2., G. Adler & A. Jaffe (Eds.). London: Routledge & Kegan Paul.

Jung, C. G. (1980). Psychology and alchemy. H. Read (Ed.), *The collected works of C. G. Jung* (R. F. C. Hall, Trans.) (CW 12). Princeton, NJ: Princeton University Press.

Jung, C. G. (1980). The Archetypes and the collective unconscious. H. Read (Ed.), *The Collected Works of C. G. Jung* (R. F. C. Hall, Trans.) (CW 9, part 1). Princeton, NJ: Princeton University Press.

Jung, C. G. (1983). Alchemical studies. H. Read (Ed.), *The Collected Works of C. G. Jung* (R. F. C. Hall, Trans.) (CW 13). Princeton, NJ: Princeton University Press.

Jung, C. G. (1984). *Selected Letters of C. G. Jung, 1909–1961.* G. Adler & A. Jaffe (Eds.). Princeton, NJ: Princeton University Press.

Jung, C. G. (1985). The practice of psychotherapy. H. Read (Ed.), *The Collected Works of C. G. Jung* (R. F. C. Hall, Trans.) (CW 16). Princeton, NJ: Princeton University Press.

Jung, C. G. (1989). Mysterium coniunctionis. H. Read (Ed.), *The Collected Works of C. G. Jung* (R. F. C. Hall, Trans.) (CW 14). Princeton, NJ: Princeton University Press.

Jung, C. G. (1991). Aion: Researches into the Phenomenology of the Self. H. Read (Ed.), *The Collected Works of C. G. Jung* (R. F. C. Hall, Trans.) (CW 9, part 11). Princeton, NJ: Princeton University Press.

Jung, C. G. (1991). Psychogenesis of mental disease. H. Read (Ed.), *The Collected Works of C. G. Jung* (R. F. C. Hall, Trans.) (CW 3). Princeton, NJ: Princeton University Press.

Jung, C. G. (1992). *Letters, 1906–1950* (Bollingen Series, XCV: 1). G. Adler, A. Jaffe (Eds.), & R. F. C Hull (Trans.). Princeton, NJ: Princeton University Press.

Kurtz, E. (1991). *Not-God: A history of Alcoholics Anonymous*. Center City, MN: Hazelden.

Lalich, J., & Langone, M. D. (2006). Characteristics of cultic groups revised. Retrieved from www.csj.org/infoserv_cult101/checklis.htm last accessed 6 March 2015.

Laney, J. (1972). *On the scholarly use of Jung's writings* (Doctoral dissertation). Jung Institute Library, Kusnacht. (Reference No. Bro 749).

Lattin, D. (2010). *The Harvard Psychedelic Club: How Timothy Leary, Ram Dass, Huston Smith and Andrew Weil Killed the Fifties and Ushered in a New Age for America*. New York, NY: HarperCollins.

Lattin, D. (2012). *Distilled Spirits: Getting High, then Sober, with a Famous Writer, a Forgotten Philosopher, and a Hopeless Drunk*. Berkeley, CA: University of California.

Le Bon, G. (2008). *The Crowd: A Study of the Popular Mind*. Digireads.com Publishing.

Le Houx, M. (2013). *Far More Than we Think: Making Sense of Spirituality*. Bloomington, IN: Balboa Press.

Lomas, R. (2010). *The Secret Science of Masonic Initiation*. San Francisco: Red Wheel/Weiser, LLC.

Mannion, P. (1991). *The Alchemical Process at Work: Analytical Psychology & Alcoholics Anonymous* (Doctoral book). C. G. Jung Library, Kusnacht, Switzerland.

McLynn, F. (1998). *Carl Gustav Jung*. New York: St. Martin's Griffin.

Melville, F. (2002). *The Book of Alchemy: The Pursuit of Wisdom and the Search for the Philosopher's Stone*. London, UK: Quantum Publishing.

Moderation Management. In: *Wikipedia the Free Encyclopedia* retrieved from http://en.wikipedia.org/wiki/Moderation_Management last accessed 6 March 2015.

Morse, R., & Flavin, D. (1992). Definition of alcoholism. *Journal of the American Medical Association, 268*: 1012–1014.

Noll, R. (1994). *The Jung Cult: Origins of a Charismatic Movement*. Princeton, NJ: Princeton University Press.

Noll, R. (1997). *The Aryan Christ: The Secret Life of Carl Jung*. New York, NY: Random House.

Peele, S., Bufe, C., & Brodsky, A. (2000). *Resisting 12-step Coercion: How to Fight Forced Participation in AA, NA, or 12-Step Treatment*. Tucson, AZ: Sharp Press.

Pittman, B. (1988). *A.A.: The Way it Began*. Seattle, WA: Glen Abbey Books.

Prochaska, J., Norcross, J. C., & DiClemente, C. C. (1994). *Changing for Good: The Revolutionary Program that Explains the Six Stages of Change and Teaches you How to Free*. New York, NY: William Morrow & Co.

Psychologist, The. (2014). Vol 27, No 9. UK: British Psychological Society. recoveryspeakers.com/rev-sam-shoemaker-his-role-in-early-aa-part-ii/ last accessed 6 March 2015.

Religious experience. (n.d.). In: *Wikipedia the Free Encyclopedia*. Retrieved from http://en.wikipedia.org/wiki/Religious_experience last accessed 6 March 2015.

Rock bottom. (2014). In: *Oxford English Dictionary*. Retrieved from www.oed.com/view/Entry/275080?redirectedFrom=rock+bottom#eid last accessed 6 March 2015.

Rosary of the philosophers. (n.d.). In: *Wikipedia, the free encyclopedia*. Retrieved from http://en.wikipedia.org/wiki/Rosary_of_the_Philosophers last accessed 6 March 2015.

Roth, S. (1973). Towards a definition of humility. *Tradition, 13*. Retrieved from www.lookstein.org/articles/humility.htm last accessed 6 March 2015.

Sacks, J. (1985). Religious issues in psychotherapy. *Journal of Religion & Health, 24*(1): 26–30.

Samuels, A., Shorter, B., & Plaut, F. (1986). *A Critical Dictionary of Jungian Analysis*. London, UK: Routledge & Kegan Paul.

Schoen, D. E. (2009). *The War of the Gods in Addiction: C. G. Jung, Alcoholics Anonymous, and Archetypal Evil*. New Orleans, LA: Spring Journal Books.

Sclater, J. E. (1993). *Carl Jung and the Path of Humility*. London, UK: Guild of Pastoral Psychology.

Shakespeare, W. (n.d.). *Complete Works of William Shakespeare: Comprising his Plays and Poems*. London, UK: Spring Books.

Shamdasani, S. (1998). *Cult fictions: C. G. Jung and the Founding of Analytical Psychology*. London, UK: Routledge.

Share, August 2013. Retrieved 20 March 2014, from www.alcoholics-anonymous.org.uk/media/Resources/Share-Magazine/August-2013/Step-Eight last accessed 6 March 2015.

Sharp, D. (1991). *C. G. Jung Lexicon: A Primer of Terms & Concepts*. Toronto, CA: Inner City Books.

Soulworks, www.soulworks.net/writings/paradigms/site_026.html last accessed 6 March 2015.

Todd, E. (1985). The value of confession and forgiveness according to Jung. *Journal of Religion and Health, 24*(1): 39–48.

Tombstone photo: www.texasdistrict5.com/history-in-photos.htm last accessed 6 March 2015.

Winners Circle: retrieved 10 March 2015. https://westcentralaa.org/PDF/ArchivedNewsletters/Jul2012.pdf

Wounded healer. (n.d.). In: *Wikipedia the Free Encyclopedia*. Retrieved from http://en.wikipedia.org/wiki/Wounded_healer last accessed 6 March 2015.

Z., P. (1990). *A Skeptic's Guide to the 12 Steps*. Center City, MN: Hazelden.

Zweig, C. (1991). *Meeting the Shadow*. Los Angeles, CA: J. P. Tarcher.

INDEX

For Product Safety Concerns and Information please contact our EU
representative GPSR@taylorandfrancis.com
Taylor & Francis Verlag GmbH, Kaufingerstraße 24, 80331 München, Germany